**The bitterest time of my slavery occurred during the first six months I lived with Covey. We worked in all weather.**

It was never too hot or too cold; it could never rain, blow, hail, or snow too hard for us to work in the fields. The longest days were too short for Covey, and the shortest nights too long for him. I was somewhat unmanageable when I first went there, but a few months of this discipline tamed me. Covey succeeded in breaking me. I was broken in body, soul, and spirit. My natural resilience was crushed, my intellect weakened, my desire to read vanished, the cheerful spark in my eye died away. The dark night of slavery closed in upon me, and I was transformed from a man to a brute.

## A Background Note about the Book

Slavery has existed in many parts of the world since ancient times. But in the American colonies, the enslavement of Africans began in the 1600s. Many of America's founding fathers, including Thomas Jefferson and George Washington, were slave owners, although both men came to believe that slavery was morally wrong. Slavery flourished in the Southern states, where large cotton and tobacco farms required the labor of many workers.

During the American Revolution (1775-1783), many Americans began to turn against slavery, believing it violated the Constitution's promise that "all men are created equal." As the 1800s began, Northern abolitionists were starting a crusade to end slavery, while Southerners insisted on their right to continue their traditional way of life, which included owning slaves.

By the time Frederick Douglass was born (probably in February 1817), slaves made up about a third of the South's population. Most were field hands, working to raise and harvest crops. Some were house slaves, working as servants in their owners' homes. They had no protection under the law of the Southern states in which they lived. They had no legal right to marry, own property, go to school, vote, testify in court, or earn their freedom. They could be bought and sold like any other piece of property.

Rising anger between the Northern and Southern states over the issue of slavery helped bring about the American Civil War. When the war ended in 1865, slavery was abolished in the United States.

# Narrative of the Life of
# FREDERICK DOUGLASS

## An American Slave

## Written by Himself

Edited, with an Afterword,
by Beth Johnson

 THE TOWNSEND LIBRARY

# Narrative of the Life of
# FREDERICK DOUGLASS

**TP** THE TOWNSEND LIBRARY

For more titles in the Townsend Library,
visit our website: **www.townsendpress.com**

All new material in this edition is
copyright © 2004 by Townsend Press.
Printed in the United States of America

9 8 7 6

Illustrations © 2004 by Hal Taylor

ISBN-13: 978-1-59194-019-7
ISBN-10: 1-59194-019-2

Library of Congress Control Number:
2003112998

# TABLE OF CONTENTS

# CHAPTER 1

I was born in Tuckahoe, near Hillsborough, in Talbot County, Maryland. I don't know my age, as I've never seen any record of my birth. In general, slaves do not know their ages any more than horses know theirs, and most masters want to keep it that way. I do not remember ever meeting a slave who could tell me his birthday. The closest most can tell is to say they were born in planting-time, harvest-time, cherry-time, spring-time, or fall-time.

Not knowing my birthday was a source of unhappiness to me during childhood. The white children knew their ages. I did not understand why I should not know mine. I was not allowed to ask my master any question about it. He thought all such questions from a slave demonstrated a restless spirit. My best guess is that I am twenty-seven or twenty-eight years old. I base this on hearing my master say, sometime in 1835, that I was about seventeen.

My mother was named Harriet Bailey. She was the daughter of Isaac and Betsy Bailey. Both of them were colored people and quite dark-skinned. My mother was of a darker complexion than either my grandmother or grandfather.

My father was a white man. That was admitted by everyone. Many people also whispered that my master was my father, but I do not know if that is true.

My mother and I were separated when I was only a baby—before I was old enough to remember anything about her. It is a common custom, in the part of Maryland from which I ran away, to separate children and their mothers at a very early age. Frequently before the child has reached its first birthday, its mother is taken away from it. She is hired out to work on a farm, miles away, and the child is placed under the care of a woman who is too old to work in the fields. Why this is done I do not know, unless it is to interfere with the natural development of affection between the mother and the child. For this is always the result.

I saw my mother only four or five times after that first separation. Each visit was very brief and at night. She was hired by a Mr. Stewart, who lived about twelve miles from my home. She made her journeys to see me in the night, walking the whole way after working all day. She was a field hand, and field hands are whipped if they are not in the field at sunrise.

I do not remember ever seeing my mother in daylight. She would lie down with me and get me to sleep, but long before I woke up she was gone. We had very little communication. Death soon ended her hardships and suffering, for she died when I was about seven years old. I was not allowed to be present during her illness, or at her death or burial. She was gone long before I knew anything about it. As I had never been allowed to know her as a mother, I heard the news of her death with the same emotions I would have felt at the death of a stranger.

When she died, she left me without the slightest idea of who my father was. The rumor that my master was my father may or may not have been true. True or not, it doesn't matter much to me. What matters is the ugly fact that the children of slave women are slaves as well. Clearly, this is to the masters' advantage. It is profitable for them to satisfy their lust with their slave women. By this arrangement, they become both master and father to a large number of valuable slaves.

It is worth noting that these slaves, with their double relationship to their master, suffer greater hardships than other slaves. They are a constant offense to their mistress. She constantly finds fault with them. She is happiest when she sees them whipped, especially when she suspects her husband of showing his mixed-race children preference over his black slaves.

The master frequently sells these slaves to please his white wife. As cruel as it may sound for a man to sell his own children, it is often the less cruel thing for him to do. For unless he does this, he must not only whip them himself, but he must stand by and see one white son tie up his brother, only a few shades darker than himself, and whip his bloody back. If the master says one word of disapproval, it is said that he is favoring his slave-child. That makes a bad matter worse, both for himself and the slave.

Every year brings with it many slaves of this class. It was because of this fact that one great Southern statesman predicted the downfall of slavery. Whether this prophecy ever comes true or not, it is plain that a very different-looking class of people are now held in slavery from those originally brought to this country from Africa. Thousands are brought into the world every year who, like myself, owe their existence to white fathers.

I have had two masters. My first master was called Captain Anthony, a title that he gained by sailing a boat on the Chesapeake Bay. He was not considered a rich slaveholder. He owned two or three farms and about thirty slaves. His property was under the care of an overseer named Plummer, a foul-mouthed and savage drunkard. Plummer always was armed with a whip and heavy club. I have known him to cut slave women's heads so horribly that Captain Anthony—who was affected by only extreme cruelty—would be enraged and threaten to whip Plummer.

Hardened by a long life of slaveholding, Captain Anthony, too, was cruel. Sometimes he took great pleasure in whipping a slave. The shrieks of my Aunt Hester often woke me at dawn. Captain Anthony would tie her up and whip her naked back until she was covered with blood. No words, no tears, no prayer from his victim softened his iron heart. The louder she screamed, the harder he whipped. Where the blood ran fastest, he whipped longest. He would whip her to make her scream and whip her to silence her. He wouldn't stop swinging the blood-clotted whip until he was exhausted.

I remember the first time I ever saw this horrible sight. I was only a small child, but I remember it well. It was the first of a long series of horrible scenes which I was forced to witness. It was my entrance to the hell of slavery, and I wish I could describe what I felt when I saw it.

This first time occurred very soon after I went to live with Captain Anthony. Aunt Hester had gone out one night, and happened to be absent when my master wanted to see her. He had ordered her not to go out in the evenings, and especially warned that she must never spend time with a certain man. This young man's name was Ned Roberts, and he belonged to Colonel Edward Lloyd. You may easily guess why Captain Anthony concerned himself with my aunt. She was a pretty woman of graceful figure. In appearance, she had very few equals among the women, colored or white, in our neighborhood.

Aunt Hester had not only disobeyed his orders in going out, but had been found with Ned. This infuriated Captain Anthony, who was himself no man of pure morals. Before he began whipping Aunt Hester, he took her into the kitchen and stripped her to the waist. He tied her hands with a strong rope, and led her to a stool under a large hook in the ceiling. He made her stand on the stool and tied her hands to the hook. Her arms were now stretched to their full length, so that she stood on her tip-toes. He then said to her, "Now, you damned bitch, I'll learn you to disobey my orders!" After rolling up his sleeves, he began to beat her with the heavy whip, and soon the warm red blood (amid heartrending shrieks from her and horrid swearing from him) came dripping to the floor. I was so terrified and horror-stricken at the sight that I hid in a closet and did not dare come out until long after the whipping was over. I expected it would be my turn next.

This was all new to me. I had always lived with my grandmother on the outskirts of the plantation, where she was placed to raise the children of the younger women. I had, until now, been away from the bloody scenes that often occurred on the plantation.

# CHAPTER 2

Captain Anthony's family included two sons, Andrew and Richard; one daughter, Lucretia; and Lucretia's husband, Captain Thomas Auld. They all lived in one house on Colonel Lloyd's plantation. Captain Anthony was Colonel Lloyd's superintendent, what might be called the overseer of the overseers. I spent two years of childhood on Colonel Lloyd's plantation, about twelve miles north of Easton, Maryland, in Talbot County.

Tobacco, corn, and wheat were the plantation's principal products. They were raised in great abundance on each of Colonel Lloyd's farms. Colonel Lloyd was able to keep a ship almost constantly busy carrying them to market in Baltimore. Captain Anthony's son-in-law, Thomas Auld, was the ship's captain. The ship was otherwise manned by four slaves whom the other slaves considered very important and very privileged because it was a great thing to be allowed to travel to Baltimore.

Colonel Lloyd kept between three and four hundred slaves on his home plantation and many more on his other farms, which numbered more than twenty. The overseers of all twenty-plus farms received instructions and advice from the managers of the home plantation, which was the great place of business and seat of government of all the farms. All disputes were settled there. Any slave who became unmanageable or showed a desire to run away was brought there and, as a warning to other slaves, was severely whipped, sent to Baltimore, and sold to a slave trader.

The slaves of all the farms received their monthly food allowance and yearly clothing at the home plantation.The adults received, as their monthly allowance, eight pounds of pork or its equivalent in fish, and one bushel of corn meal. Their yearly clothing consisted of two coarse linen shirts, one pair of linen trousers, one jacket, one pair of winter trousers, one pair of stockings, and one pair of shoes. The whole wardrobe could not have cost more than seven dollars. The children too young to work in the fields had neither shoes, stockings, jackets, or trousers. Their clothing consisted of two coarse linen shirts per year. When these wore out, they went naked until the next allowance day.

The slaves were given no beds, unless one coarse blanket counts as a bed, and only the adults had these. This, however, is not considered a great problem. The lack of a bed creates less difficulty for a slave than the lack of time to sleep. For when the day's work in the field is done, most of them have their washing, mending, and cooking to do. As they have few of the tools needed to do any of these chores, many of their sleeping hours are used preparing for the coming day. When this is done, they drop down side-by-side—old and young, male and female, married and single—on the cold, damp floor, each covering himself or herself with a miserable blanket. Here they sleep until they are summoned to the field by the sound of the horn.

At this sound, all must rise and be off to the field. There must be no delay. Trouble awaits those who do not hear the morning alarm! For if they are not awakened by the sense of hearing, they are by the sense of feeling. Mr. Severe, the overseer, used to stand by the door of the slave quarters, ready to whip anyone who was so unfortunate as not to hear.

Mr. Severe was well-named, for he was a

cruel man. I have seen him whip a woman, causing her blood to run for half an hour at a time, in the midst of her crying children. Added to his cruelty was his dreadful swearing. It was enough to chill the blood to hear him talk. Hardly a sentence escaped him that didn't include some horrid oath. His presence made the workplace a field of blood and blasphemy. From the rising of the sun until it set, he was cursing, raving, cutting, and slashing among the slaves in the most frightful manner. His career was short. He died very soon after I went to Colonel Lloyd's. He died as he lived, uttering bitter curses and horrid oaths. The slaves regarded his death as the act of a merciful God.

Mr. Severe's place was filled by a man named Mr. Hopkins. He was very different. He was less cruel, less profane, and made less noise than Mr. Severe. He whipped, but did not seem to take pleasure in it. The slaves called him a good overseer.

The home plantation of Colonel Lloyd looked like a country village. The mechanical operations for all the farms were performed here, including the shoemaking and mending, blacksmithing, cartwrighting, weaving, and grain-grinding. The slaves called it the Great House Farm, and it was considered a great privilege to be sent to do errands there. Slaves working in the outlying farms would do anything to prove themselves smart and trustworthy, so that their overseers would select them for such tasks, and be, for that time, away from the fields and the slave driver's whip.

Slaves especially wanted to be selected to go to the Great House Farm to pick up the monthly allowances for themselves and their fellow slaves. While on their way, they would make the forests around them echo with their songs. They would make up the songs as they went along.

When I was a slave, I did not understand the deep meaning of these crude, simple songs. I was myself within the circle of slavery, so that I did not see or hear things as I would if I were outside it. But these songs told a tale of sadness that was beyond my feeble understanding. They breathed the prayer of souls boiling over with bitter anguish. Every note was a testimony against slavery and a prayer to God for deliverance from chains. Even now, remembering those songs affects me deeply. While I write these lines, tears are running down my cheeks. If anyone wants to understand the soul-killing effects of slavery, let him go to Colonel Lloyd's plantation on allowance day, hide himself in the deep pine woods, and listen.

I have often been astonished, since I came to the North, to hear people say that the singing of slaves is evidence of their happiness. It is impossible to imagine a greater mistake. Slaves sing most when they are most unhappy. The songs of the slave represent the sorrow of his heart. He is relieved by his songs, as an aching heart is relieved by tears. A man cast away on a desert island might sing, and no one would consider that evidence of his happiness. The songs of the castaway and the slave are prompted by the same emotion.

# ⋆ CHAPTER 3

Colonel Lloyd kept a large, fine garden, which kept four men and the chief gardener almost constantly busy. The garden was probably the greatest attraction of the place. In the summer, people came from as far away as Baltimore and Annapolis to see it. It contained fruits of almost every kind, from the hardy apple of the north to the delicate orange of the south. The garden was a source of great trouble on the plantation. Its excellent fruit was quite a temptation to the hungry swarms of boys, as well as the older slaves. Hardly a day passed during the summer but that some slave was whipped for stealing fruit.

The colonel tried all kinds of tricks to keep his slaves out of the garden. The last and most successful one was to spread tar all over the fence that surrounded it. After that, if a slave was caught with any tar on himself, it was considered proof that he had tried to enter the garden, and he was severely whipped by the chief gardener. This plan worked well, as the slaves became as fearful of tar as of the whip.

The colonel also kept a splendid collection of horses and carriages. The horses were of the finest form and noblest blood. His carriage-house contained three splendid large coaches, three or four small two-wheeled carriages, plus several other vehicles of the latest fashion.

The carriage-house was cared for by two slaves: a father and son, Old Barney and Young Barney. This was their only work. But their job was not easy, for Colonel Lloyd was extremely particular about his horses. The slightest neglect of them was unpardonable, and the colonel constantly suspected such neglect. This, of course, made Old and Young Barney's jobs very difficult. They never knew when they were safe from punishment. They were frequently whipped when they didn't deserve it, and escaped whipping when they did.

Everything depended on the looks of the horses, and the state of Colonel Lloyd's mind when the horses were brought to him. If a horse did not move fast enough, or hold his head high enough, it was the keepers' fault. It was painful to stand near the stable door and hear his complaints against the keepers. "This horse has not had proper attention. He has not been rubbed or combed enough, or he has not been properly fed. His food is too wet or too dry. He was fed too early or too late. He is too hot or too cold; he has had too much hay and not enough grain; he has had too much grain and not enough hay." Instead of Old Barney caring for the horse, he very improperly left it to Young Barney.

To all these complaints, no matter how unfair, the slave must never answer a word. Colonel Lloyd could not bear any contradiction from a slave. When he spoke, a slave must stand, listen, and tremble. I have seen Colonel Lloyd make Old Barney, a man between fifty and sixty years of age, uncover his bald head, kneel down upon the cold, damp ground, and receive upon his work-worn shoulders more than thirty lashes of the whip.

Colonel Lloyd had three sons and three sons-in-law. All six lived at the Great House Farm, and were allowed to whip the servants when they pleased, from Old Barney down to the coach driver.

It would be almost impossible to describe the riches of Colonel Lloyd. He kept from ten to fifteen house servants, and he was said to own a thousand slaves. Colonel Lloyd owned so many that he did not know them when he saw them, nor did all the slaves living on the outlying farms know him. People say that while riding along the road one day, the colonel met a colored man. He spoke to him in the way white men usually did in the South: "Well, boy, whom do you belong to?"

"To Colonel Lloyd," replied the slave.

"And does the colonel treat you well?" he asked.

"No, sir," was the reply.

"Does he work you too hard?" asked the colonel.

"Yes, sir."

"Well, don't he give you enough to eat?"

"Yes, sir; he gives me enough, such as it is," the slave answered.

The colonel rode on, and the man also went on about his business, not dreaming that he had been talking with his master. He heard nothing more of the matter until two or three weeks afterward. The poor man was then told by his overseer that, as punishment for criticizing his master, he was being sold to a Georgia slave trader. He was immediately chained and handcuffed and, without a moment's warning, snatched away from his family and friends. This is the penalty of telling the truth to a series of plain questions.

As a result of such incidents, when slaves are asked about their condition and the character of their master, they almost always say they are contented and that their masters are kind. The slaveholders have been known to send spies in among their slaves to ask such questions. When I was a slave, I was frequently asked if I had a kind master. I always said yes. Furthermore, I did not think that I was absolutely lying, for I judged my master against the slaveholders around us.

Slaves are like other people, and they have their own prejudices. They like to believe that their own masters are better than the masters of other slaves, even when the very reverse is true. Slaves will even quarrel among themselves, each arguing that his master is better than that of the other man's. It was so on our plantation. When Colonel Lloyd's slaves met the slaves of Jacob Jepson, they seldom parted without a quarrel about their masters. Colonel Lloyd's slaves would claim that he was the richest, and Mr. Jepson's slaves would say that he was the smartest, and more of a man. Colonel Lloyd's slaves would boast of his ability to buy and sell Jacob Jepson. Mr. Jepson's slaves would boast of his ability to whip Colonel Lloyd.

These quarrels would almost always end

in a fight, and the slaves that won were supposed to have proved their point. They seemed to think that the greatness of their master was somehow transferred to themselves. It was considered bad enough to be a slave, but to be a poor man's slave was a disgrace indeed!

# CHAPTER 4

Mr. Hopkins did not last very long as overseer. Why his career was so short I do not know, but I suppose he was not strict enough to suit Colonel Lloyd. After Mr. Hopkins came Mr. Austin Gore, a man who had every quality his employer could wish. Mr. Gore had worked for Colonel Lloyd on one of the out-farms, and had shown himself worthy of the important job of overseer at Great House Farm.

Mr. Gore was proud and ambitious. He was also clever, cruel, and stubborn. He was just the man for such a place. He was one of those who could see rudeness in the slightest look, word, or gesture from a slave, and he would treat it accordingly.

There must be no answering back to him. A slave was never allowed any explanation to show that he had been wrongfully accused. Mr. Gore fully believed the slaveholder's rule: "It is better to whip a dozen slaves wrongfully than to let the slaves see that the overseer has made a mistake." It didn't matter how innocent a slave might be, once he had been accused by Mr. Gore of any fault. To be accused was to be found guilty, and to be found guilty was to be punished. The only way to escape punishment was to escape accusation, and few slaves managed that under Mr. Gore's supervision. He was, of all the overseers, the most dreaded by the slaves. His presence was painful; his glance created confusion all around him; and his sharp, shrill voice produced horror and trembling among them.

Although Mr. Gore was a young man, he indulged in no jokes, made no funny remarks, and seldom smiled. His words were in perfect keeping with his looks, and his looks were in perfect keeping with his words. Overseers will sometimes indulge in a witty word, even with the slaves, but not so with Mr. Gore. He spoke only to command, and commanded to be obeyed. He was stingy with his words, and generous with his whip, and he never used the former when the latter would do.

His savage barbarity was equaled only by the coolness with which he committed the most savage deeds upon the slaves under his supervision. Mr. Gore once began to whip one of Colonel Lloyd's slaves, by the name of

Demby. He had given Demby only a few stripes when, to ease the pain, Demby ran and plunged himself into a creek. He stood there in water up to his shoulders, refusing to come out.

Mr. Gore told him that he would count to three, and if he did not come out, he would shoot him. Mr. Gore began to count. Demby made no answer, but stood his ground. The counting continued with no response from Demby. Without a word to anyone, Mr. Gore then raised his rifle, took deadly aim at his standing victim, and in an instant poor Demby was no more. His mangled body sank out of sight, and blood and brains marked the water where he had stood.

A shudder of horror flashed through every soul upon the plantation, excepting Mr. Gore. He seemed cool and collected. He was asked by Colonel Lloyd and my old master why he had taken this extraordinary action. His reply was that Demby had become unmanageable. He was setting a dangerous example to the other slaves—one which, if allowed to pass, would lead to the end of rule and order on the plantation. He argued that if one slave refused to be corrected, and escaped with his life, the other slaves would soon copy his example. The result, said Mr. Gore, would be the freedom of the slaves and enslavement of the whites.

Mr. Gore's explanation satisfied them. He kept his job, and became widely known as an excellent overseer. He was not even charged with a crime. It was committed in the presence of slaves, and they of course could not bring charges against him, or even testify against him. And so the perpetrator of a bloody, foul murder goes unpunished and uncriticized by his own community. Gore lived in St. Michael's, Talbot County, Maryland, when I left there. He probably lives there now, as much respected as if his soul had not been stained with his brother's blood.

In Talbot County killing a slave, or any other black, is not treated as a crime. Thomas Lanman, of St. Michael's, killed two slaves. He killed one with a hatchet, knocking his brains out. He used to boast about the awful deed. I have heard him laugh as he did so, saying that others should thank him and do as he had done; that way, the country soon would be rid of "the damned niggers."

The wife of Mr. Giles Hicks, who lived near where I used to live, murdered my wife's cousin, a girl of only fifteen or sixteen. She mangled the poor girl in the most horrible manner, so that she lived only a few hours.

The victim was immediately buried, but had been in her untimely grave only a few hours before she was dug up and examined by the coroner, who decided that she had been killed by a severe beating.

This is what happened. She had been told to mind Mrs. Hicks's baby, and during the night she fell asleep and the baby cried. She had not slept for several nights, and did not hear the crying. She and the infant were both in the room with Mrs. Hicks. When Mrs. Hicks found the girl slow to move, she jumped from her bed, seized a stick of wood by the fireplace, and beat the girl with it, breaking her nose and breastbone. I will not say that this horrid murder did not scandalize the community. It did create a scandal, but not enough to bring the murderess to punishment. A warrant was issued for her arrest, but it was never served. She escaped punishment, and even the pain of being brought before a court.

While I am telling of bloody deeds which took place during my stay on Colonel Lloyd's plantation, I will briefly tell of one more, which occurred about the same time as the murder of Demby by Mr. Gore.

Colonel Lloyd's slaves were in the habit of spending a part of their nights and Sundays fishing for oysters, so as to make up for their scanty diet. An old man belonging to Colonel Lloyd was oystering, and happened to wander beyond the limits of Colonel Lloyd's property and onto the property of Mr. Beal Bondly. Mr. Bondly took offense at this trespass, came down to the shore with his rifle, and shot the poor old man dead.

Mr. Bondly came over to see Colonel Lloyd the next day. I don't know whether he came to pay him for his property, or to justify what he had done. At any rate, the whole devilish act was soon hushed up. There was very little said about it at all, and nothing done. It was a common saying, even among the little white boys, that it was worth a half-penny to kill a "nigger," and half-penny to bury one.

# CHAPTER 5

My own treatment while I lived on Colonel Lloyd's plantation was similar to that of the other slave children. I was not old enough to work in the fields, and as there was little besides field work to do, I had a great deal of leisure time.

The most I had to do was to drive the cows home at evening, keep the chickens out of the garden, keep the front yard clean, and run errands for Captain Anthony's daughter, Lucretia Auld. I spent most of my leisure time helping Colonel Lloyd's young son Daniel find birds after he shot them. My connection with Daniel Lloyd was an advantage to me. He became fond of me and protected me. He would not allow the older boys to bother me, and he divided his cakes with me.

Captain Anthony seldom whipped me. My greatest sufferings were produced by hunger and cold—especially cold. In hottest summer and coldest winter, I was kept almost naked. I had no shoes, no stockings, no jacket, no trousers—nothing but a coarse linen shirt which reached to my knees. I had no bed. I would have died from cold, but on the coldest nights I used to steal a bag that was used for carrying corn to the mill. I would crawl into this bag, then sleep on the cold, damp, clay floor, with my head inside the bag and my feet out. My feet were sometimes so cracked with the frost that I could lay the pen with which I am now writing in the deep gashes.

Our food was coarse corn meal, boiled into mush. It was put into a large wooden trough and set down on the ground. The children were then called, as though we were pigs, and like pigs we would come to devour the mush. Some ate with their bare hands, some used oyster shells, others a piece of shingle, but none ate with spoons. He that ate fastest got the most, and he that was strongest got the best place at the trough. Few left with their hunger satisfied.

I probably was seven or eight years old when I left Colonel Lloyd's plantation. I'll never forget the joy with which I learned that Captain Anthony had decided to let me go to Baltimore. There I would live with Hugh

Auld, the brother of Captain Anthony's son-in-law, Thomas Auld. I learned this about three days before my departure.

During those three days, I spent most of my time in the creek, washing off the dirt of the plantation and preparing myself for departure. I washed because Lucretia Auld told me that I had to remove all the dead skin from my feet and knees before I could go to Baltimore. She said that the people in Baltimore were very clean and would laugh at me if I looked dirty. Besides, she was going to give me a pair of trousers, which I shouldn't put on until I had removed all the dirt. The thought of owning a pair of trousers was great indeed. It motivated me to scrub until I had removed not only the dirt but almost my skin.

The ties that ordinarily bind children to their homes did not exist in my case. I felt no sadness at the thought of leaving. I was not leaving any loved one. My mother was dead. My grandmother lived far away, so I seldom saw her. I had two sisters and one brother who lived in the same house as I, but our early separation from our mother had made us nearly forget that we were related.

My cousin Tom had described Baltimore in a way that made me wild with desire to see it. Whenever I had pointed out something beautiful or fine at Great House Farm, Tom had told me that he had seen something far more beautiful or fine in Baltimore.

We sailed for Baltimore on a Saturday morning. I remember only the day of the week because I did not know the days of the month then, or the months of the year. From the ship's deck I looked back at Colonel Lloyd's plantation for what I hoped would be the last time.

Early on Sunday morning we landed at Smith's Wharf, in Baltimore. A large flock of sheep was on board. After I helped drive the sheep to a slaughterhouse, a ship hand showed me to my new home. It was on Alliciana Street, in the section called Fell's Point.

Hugh and Sophia Auld met me at the door with their little son Thomas. I saw what I never had seen before: a white face beaming with kindness. This was the face of Sophia Auld. Happiness flashed through my soul. Thomas was told that this was his Freddy, and I was told to take care of Thomas. I entered into the duties of my new home in a most cheerful frame of mind.

My departure from Colonel Lloyd's plantation was one of the most important events of my life. If it hadn't been for this departure, I might have remained a slave. Instead I am sitting here at my table, enjoying freedom and the happiness of my own home, writing this story. Going to live in Baltimore laid the foundation for everything that would follow.

I have always seen it as the first plain sign of the kindness with which God has treated me, and marked my life with so many favors. That I was chosen to go to Baltimore is a remarkable thing. There were a number of slave children that might have been sent in my place. But I was chosen from among them all.

I may be called superstitious, and even egotistical, in seeing this event as an act of God in my favor. But I would be lying to my own soul if I did not state my opinion. For as long as I can remember, I held the deepest belief that slavery would not be able to hold me in its filthy embrace forever. In the darkest hours of my slavery, this spirit of hope stayed with me like a ministering angel. This good spirit was from God, and to him I offer thanksgiving and praise.

# CHAPTER 6

Sophia Auld turned out to be all that she had appeared to be at our first meeting—a woman of the kindest heart and feelings. Having a slave under her control was new to her. Before her marriage she had made her own living. A weaver by trade, she had been almost entirely shielded from slavery's dehumanizing effects. Because she was unlike any other white woman I had known, I was uncertain how to act toward her. When I behaved in a humble, crouching way, it disturbed, rather than pleased, her. She did not think it was rude for a slave to look her in the face. Her smiles were heavenly and her voice peaceful.

Soon after I went to live in Baltimore, Sophia Auld kindly taught me the alphabet. After that, she helped me to spell three- and four-letter words. But then Hugh Auld discovered what was going on and insisted that his wife stop teaching me. He told her, among other things, that it was unlawful and unsafe to teach a slave to read. "If you give a nigger an inch, they will take a mile," he said. "Niggers should know nothing other than how to do as they're told." Pointing to me, he said, "If you teach that nigger to read, he will be spoiled as a slave. He will become unmanageable and of no value to his master. It will harm *him* as well; it will make him discontented."

These words sank deep into my heart, stirring up thoughts that had until then lain asleep. They explained things that I had not understood before. I now understood the white man's power to enslave the black man. From this moment, I understood the pathway from slavery to freedom. It was just what I wanted, and I got it when I least expected it. While I was sad at the thought of losing the aid of my kind mistress, I was glad to have learned, quite by accident, something of great worth from my master.

Although I realized the difficulty of learning without a teacher, I set out with great determination to learn how to read. The very firmness with which Mr. Auld spoke convinced me that he deeply believed the truth of what he was saying. What he most dreaded, I most desired. What he most loved, I most hated. That which was to him a great evil, to be carefully avoided, was to me a great good, to be earnestly sought. His arguments only served to inspire me. In learning to read, I owe almost as much to the opposition of my master as to the kindly aid of my mistress.

Soon after I moved to Baltimore I became aware of a great difference in the treatment of slaves from that which I had seen in the country. A city slave is almost a freeman compared with a plantation slave. He is much better fed and clothed, and enjoys privileges unknown to the slave on the plantation. There is a shred of decency and a sense of shame that discourages those outbreaks of cruelty so common on the plantation. Only the most evil slaveholder is willing to shock his non-slaveholding neighbors with the cries of his beaten slave. Few are willing to put up with the shame attached to the reputation of being a cruel master. Above all, they do not want to be known for not giving a slave enough to eat. Every city slaveholder is anxious to have people say that he feeds his slaves well, and most of them do so.

There are, however, some painful exceptions to this rule. Directly opposite us, on Philpot Street, lived Mr. Thomas Hamilton. He owned two slaves, Henrietta and Mary. Henrietta was about twenty-two years old,

Mary was about fourteen, and of all the mangled, emaciated creatures I ever saw, they were the most pitiful. A person who could look at those two and not feel moved must have a heart harder than stone.

Mary's head, neck, and shoulders were literally cut to pieces by the whip of her cruel mistress. I do not know if her master ever whipped her, but I used to be in their house nearly every day, and I have been an eyewitness to the cruelty of Mrs. Hamilton. Mrs. Hamilton used to sit in a large chair in the middle of the room, with a heavy whip always by her side, and hardly an hour went by that she did not draw blood from one of these slaves.

The girls seldom passed without her saying, "Move faster, you black trash!" at the same time hitting them with the whip on the head or shoulders, often drawing blood. She would then say, "Take that, you black trash! If you don't move faster, I'll move you!" Added to the cruel beatings which these slaves suffered, they were kept nearly half-starved. They seldom knew what it was to eat a full meal. I have seen Mary compete with the pigs for the garbage thrown into the street.

# CHAPTER 7

I lived in Master Hugh's family for about seven years. During this time, I succeeded in learning to read and write. To accomplish this, I had to use various tricks. I had no regular teacher. My mistress, who had kindly begun to instruct me, had (in obedience to her husband) not only stopped instructing me, but had set her face against my being instructed by anyone else. To be fair, she did not adopt this course of treatment immediately. She at first lacked the evil qualities necessary to shut me up in mental darkness. It was necessary for her to be taught to use irresponsible power before she was able to treat me as though I were an animal.

My mistress was, as I have said, a kind and tenderhearted woman. In the basic goodness of her soul she began, when I first went to live with her, to treat me as she believed one human being ought to treat another. As she began to exercise her duties as a slaveholder, she did not seem to understand that I was merely a piece of property. And she did not realize that for her to treat me as a human being was not only wrong, but dangerous.

Slavery proved to be as harmful to her as it was to me. When I went there, she was a pious, warm woman. There was no sorrow or suffering for which she did not shed a tear. She had bread for the hungry, clothes for the naked, and comfort for every mourner that came within her reach.

But slavery soon proved its ability to strip her of these heavenly qualities. Under its influence, the tender heart became stone, and the lamb-like personality gave way to one of tiger-like fierceness.

The first step in her downward course was in her ceasing to instruct me. She then began to carry out her husband's beliefs, and she became even more convinced of those opinions than he himself. She was not satisfied with simply doing what he had commanded; she seemed anxious to do more. Nothing seemed to make her more angry than to see me with a newspaper. I have had her rush at me with a face full of fury, and snatch the newspaper from me, in a way that fully revealed her terror. She was a clever woman, and a little experience soon taught her the truth: that education and slavery were incompatible with each other.

From this time I was most carefully watched. If I was in a separate room for any length of time, I was sure to be suspected of having a book, and was at once called to explain myself. All this, however, was too late. The first step had been taken. Mistress, in teaching me the alphabet, had given me the inch. No precaution could prevent me from taking the mile.

The plan which I adopted was that of making friends with all the little white boys whom I met in the street. I convinced many of them to become my teachers. With their kindly aid, given at different times and in different places, I finally succeeded in learning to read. When I was sent on errands, I always took my book with me. By doing the errand quickly, I found time to get a lesson before my return. I used to carry bread with me, for I was better off in this regard than many of the poor white children in the neighborhood. This bread I used to give to the hungry little urchins, and in return, they would give me the more valuable bread of knowledge.

I am strongly tempted to name two or three of those little boys, as an expression of the gratitude and affection I feel for them. But good sense stops me. It is not that it would injure me, but it might embarrass them, for it is almost an unforgivable offense to teach slaves to read in this Christian country. It is enough to say that the dear little fellows lived on Philpot Street.

I used to talk the matter of slavery over with them. I would sometimes say to them that I wished I could be as free as they would be when they got to be men. "You will be free as soon as you are twenty-one," I would say, "*but I am a slave for life*! Don't I have as much right to be free as you?" These words used to trouble them. They would express their lively sympathy, and comfort me with the hope that something would happen, and that I might someday be free.

I was now about twelve years old, and the thought of being a slave for life began to weigh heavily on my heart. Just about this time, I got hold of a book called *The Columbian Orator*. Every opportunity I got, I used to read this book. Among many interesting stories, I found a dialogue between a master and his slave. The slave had run away from his master three times. The dialogue was supposed to be the conversation which took place between them when the slave was recaptured for the third time. In this dialogue, the master made all his arguments on behalf of slavery, and the slave pointed out the wrongness of each of these points. What the slave had to say was most intelligent and impressive, and it had such an effect that the master freed him on the spot.

This was a marvelous document to me. The moral which I took from it was that truth had power even over the conscience of a slaveowner. The more I read of this and other material, the more I grew to detest my enslavers. I could see them as nothing but a band of successful robbers who had left their homes, gone to Africa, and stolen us from our homes in order to bring us to a strange land and reduce us to slavery. I hated them as the lowest and most wicked of men.

As I read and thought, that dissatisfaction which Mr. Auld had predicted came into being, tormenting and stinging my soul. As I suffered, I at times felt that learning to read had been a curse rather than a blessing. It had given me a view of my wretched condition, but no cure. It opened my eyes to the horrible pit, but gave me no ladder with which to get out. In moments of agony, I envied my fellow slaves for their ignorance. I often wished myself an animal. I preferred the life of a lowest reptile to my own. Anything, no matter what, to get rid of this thinking! It was this everlasting thinking about my condition that tormented me.

But there was no getting rid of it. The silver trumpet of freedom had wakened my soul. Freedom now appeared, and would never disappear again. It was heard in every sound, and seen in every thing. It was ever present, tormenting me with a sense of my miserable condition. It looked from every star, it smiled in every calm, breathed in every wind, and moved in every storm.

I often found myself wishing myself dead. Except for the hope of being free, I no doubt would have killed myself, or done something for which I would have been killed.

While I was in this state of mind, I was eager to hear anyone speak about slavery. Every so often, I would hear something about the "abolitionists." It was some time before I found out what the word meant. It was always used in a way that interested me. If a slave ran away and succeeded in escaping, or if a slave killed his master, set fire to a barn, or did anything very wrong in the mind of a slaveholder, it was blamed on abolition. Wanting to learn what this word meant, I went to the dictionary. It gave me little help. I found out "abolition" meant "the act of abolishing, or getting rid of" but I did not know what was to be abolished. I was puzzled. I did not dare ask anyone about its meaning, for I was sure it was something my masters did not want me to know about.

After a long wait, I got hold of a newspaper that contained a story about Northern demands for the abolition of slavery in the District of Columbia. From this I began to understand what *abolition* and *abolitionist* meant. I always drew near when those words were spoken, expecting to hear something of importance to me and my fellow slaves.

The light broke in upon me by degrees. One day, down on the wharf, I saw two Irishmen unloading stone. I went, unasked, and helped them. When we had finished, one of them asked if I were a slave. I told him I was. He asked, "Are ye a slave for life?" I told him that I was. The good Irishman seemed deeply affected. He said to the other that it was a pity so fine a little fellow as myself should be a slave for life, and that it was a shame to hold me. They both advised me to run away to the north; that I should find friends there, and that I should be free.

I pretended not to be interested, and acted as if I did not understand. I feared they might betray me. White men have been known to encourage slaves to escape and then, to get the reward, catch them and return them to their masters. I was afraid that these seemingly good men might do that, but I still remembered their advice. I looked forward to a time when it would be safe for me to escape. I was too young to think of doing so immediately. Besides, I wanted to learn how to write, so that I could someday forge my own freeman's papers. I comforted myself with the hope that I would one day find a good chance to go. Meanwhile, I would learn to write.

The idea of how I might do that came to me as I watched the carpenters working in the shipyard. After cutting a piece of timber, they would write on it the part of the ship for which it was intended. A piece meant for the larboard side, for instance, was marked "L." A piece for the starboard side was marked "S." A piece for the larboard side forward was marked "L.F." and so on. I began copying these letters and within a short time could write them. After that, when I met with a boy who I knew could write, I would tell him I could write as well as he. His next words would be, "I don't believe you. Let me see you try." I would then make the letters, and ask him to beat that. In this way I got a good many lessons in writing, which I would never have gotten any other way.

During this time, my copybook was the board fence, brick wall, and pavement. My pen and ink was a lump of chalk. With these, I learned the basics of writing. I then began copying words out of Webster's *Spelling Book*, until I could write them all without looking at the book. By this time, my little Thomas Auld had gone to school and learned to write. He had brought home his copybooks, which had been shown to some of our neighbors and then laid aside. My mistress used to go out every Monday afternoon, and leave me to take care of the house. When I was left there, I used to spend the time writing in the spaces left in Thomas Auld's copybook, copying what he had written. And so, after a long, tedious effort of many years, I learned to write.

# CHAPTER 8

Soon after I went to live in Baltimore, my old master's youngest son, Richard, died. About three and a half years after that, my old master, Captain Anthony, died. That left only his son, Andrew, and daughter, Lucretia, to share his estate. He had died suddenly, leaving no will concerning the disposal of his property. It was therefore necessary to have the property evaluated, so that it might be equally divided between his two children. I was immediately sent for, to be valued with the other property.

I left Baltimore with a young heart full of sadness, and a soul full of anxiety. After a sail of nearly twenty-four hours, I found myself near the place of my birth. I had been absent from it almost five years. I was between ten and eleven.

We were all ranked together at the evaluation. There were horses and men, cattle and women, pigs and children, all holding the same importance, and all subject to the same examination. Silver-headed elders and lively youths, maids and matrons, had to undergo the same shameful inspection. At this moment, I saw more clearly than ever the brutalizing effects of slavery upon both slave and slaveholder.

After the valuation, then came the division. I have no language to express the anxiety which we poor slaves felt during this time. Our fate for life was now to be decided. We had no more say in the decision than the beasts among whom we were classified. A single word from the white men was enough to separate forever the strongest ties known to human beings. In addition to the pain of separation, there was the dread of falling into the hands of Master Andrew. He was known to us all as a cruel wretch—a common drunkard who had, by his reckless mismanagement, already wasted a large portion of his father's property.

I suffered more anxiety than most of my fellow slaves. I had known what it was to be kindly treated; they had known nothing of the sort. They had seen little or nothing of the world. Their backs had been familiar with the bloody lash, and had become tough; mine was still tender, for in Baltimore I got few whippings, and few slaves had a kinder master or mistress than myself. The thought of going from their home into the hands of Master Andrew terrified me. This was a man who, only a few days before, had taken my little brother by the throat, thrown him on the ground, and stamped on his head with the heel of his boot until the blood gushed from his nose and ears. After he had so savagely assaulted my brother, he turned to me and said he would do the same to me one of these days—meaning, I supposed, when I became his possession.

Thanks be to God, I was assigned to Lucretia Auld's portion of property, and was sent immediately back to Baltimore. Hugh Auld's family was as happy to see me return as they had been sad to see me go. It was a glad day for me. I had escaped a fate worse than the lion's jaws. I was absent from Baltimore just about one month, although it seemed to me at least six.

Soon after my return to Baltimore, Lucretia Auld died. Soon after her death, Master Andrew also died. Of all the slaves who had belonged to Captain Anthony and then to his children, not a single one was freed. I remained the property of Thomas Auld, Lucretia's widower.

At this time the shameful treatment of my

grandmother deepened my hatred of slavery and slaveholders. From youth to old age, she had served Captain Anthony faithfully. Having populated his plantation with slaves, she had been a primary source of his wealth. She had rocked him in his infancy, cared for him in his childhood, served him throughout his life, and at his death wiped the sweat from his brow and closed his eyes. Yet, both Captain Anthony and his children had left her a slave—for life. She saw strangers divide up her children, grandchildren, and great-grand-children like so many sheep.

Being very old, my grandmother was of little value to her new owners; her body was racked with pains, and helplessness was steal-ing over her once strong limbs. So her owners built a little hut in the woods and left her there to care for herself in utter loneliness. In effect, they turned her out to die. If my poor grandmother still is alive, she lives only to remember and mourn the loss of her children, grandchildren, and great-grandchildren. Her home is cold and empty. Instead of her fami-ly's voices, she hears the dove's moan by day and the owl's scream by night. Now, when she most needs her children's tenderness and affection, this devoted mother of twelve is alone before a cold fireplace. No one is there to even give her a decent burial.

About two years after his wife Lucretia died, Thomas Auld married Rowena Hamilton. Soon after the marriage, Thomas Auld argued with his brother Hugh. To punish his brother, Thomas Auld took me to live at his house in St. Michael's.

I was not sorry to leave Hugh and Sophia Auld. They had greatly changed. Brandy's influence on him and slavery's influence on her had disastrously affected their characters. However, I was sorry to leave the little Baltimore boys who had given me many good lessons. I also regretted that I had not tried to run away; the chances of success are ten times greater from the city than from the country.

So I sailed from Baltimore for St. Michael's. During the trip I paid special attention to the route that steamboats took to Philadelphia. When they reached North Point, they went up the bay, in a northeasterly direction, instead of going south. This was important information. My determination to run away had been revived. As soon as I had a good chance, I would try to escape.

# CHAPTER 9

I have now reached the period of my life when I can give dates. I left Baltimore, and went to live with Master Thomas Auld, at St. Michael's, in March, 1832. It was now more than seven years since I had lived with him on Colonel Lloyd's plantation. Of course, by now we were almost complete strangers to each other. I knew nothing about his temper or character, nor he of mine. In a very short time, however, we were well acquainted. I grew to know his wife as well as himself. They were a well-matched pair, being equally cruel.

Now, for the first time in more than seven years, I experienced hunger. It had been hard enough to bear when I was a child, but it was ten times worse now, after living in Hugh Auld's house, where I had always had enough good food to eat. Even among slaveowners, it is considered wrong not to give a slave enough to eat. The rule is, no matter how plain the food, at least let there be enough of it. Thomas Auld did not give us enough even of the poorest food.

There were four of us slaves in the kitchen—my sister Eliza, my aunt Priscilla, Henny, and myself—and we were given less than half a bushel of cornmeal a week, and very little else. It was not enough to survive upon. We therefore were forced to live at the expense of our neighbors. This we did by begging and stealing, whichever was more handy. Many times we were nearly dead with hunger, when food lay spoiling in the storehouse, and yet every morning Thomas and Rowena Auld would kneel and pray that God would bless them more abundantly!

Bad as all slaveholders are, most have at least one good quality. Thomas Auld was the exception. I do not know of one kind or generous act that he ever performed. He was not born a slaveholder. He had been a poor man, captain only of one small ship. He came into possession of his slaves through marriage, and of all men, newly-made slaveholders were the worst. He was cruel, but cowardly. He commanded without firmness. In enforcing his rules, he was sometimes rigid, and sometimes lazy. Sometimes he spoke to his slaves with the fury of a demon; at other times, he might have been mistaken for a traveler who had lost his way. He did no work himself.

The luxury of having slaves was something new, and he was unprepared for it. We seldom called him "master." Instead, we called him "Captain Auld," when we called him anything at all. Our lack of respect for him must have puzzled him greatly. He wanted us to call him master, but lacked the dignity that would have caused us to do so. His wife tried to insist upon us calling him by that name, but with no effect.

In August 1832, Thomas Auld attended a Methodist camp meeting, and there he got religion. I briefly hoped that his conversion would lead him to free his slaves or, at least, make him more kind and humane. I was disappointed on both scores. If it had any effect on his character, it made him more cruel and hateful than ever. Before his conversion, he relied upon his own cruelty, but after it, he found religious grounds to support his behavior.

He made a great show of being a pious man. His house was the house of prayer, and he prayed morning, noon, and night. He soon became well-known among his neighbors as a powerful man of God. His house was the preachers' favorite. They used to take great pleasure in visiting him, for while he starved us, he stuffed them. We often had three or four preachers staying there at one time.

While I lived with my master in St. Michael's, there was a young white man, a Mr. Wilson, who offered to start a Sunday school for the instruction of slaves who might wish to learn to read the New Testament. We met only three times, when white neighbors of Thomas Auld burst in upon us with sticks and other weapons, drove us off, and forbade us to meet again. And so ended our little Sunday school in the godly town of St. Michael's.

Thomas Auld found excuses for his cruelty in religion. As an example, I will tell you that I have seen him tie up a lame young woman, Henny, and whip her upon her naked shoulders, causing the warm red blood to drip. To justify this bloody deed, he quoted this passage of Scripture: "He that knoweth his master's will, and doeth it not, shall be beaten with many stripes." I have known him to tie her up early in the morning and whip her before breakfast, leave her, go to his store, return at dinner, and whip her again, cutting her in the places he had already made raw with his whip.

The secret of his cruelty toward Henny lay in the fact that she was almost helpless. When she was a child, she fell into the fire and burned herself horribly. Her hands were so injured that they were useless. She could do little besides carry heavy loads. She was an expense to Thomas Auld, and because he was a stingy man, this greatly offended him. He once gave her away to his sister but, as she was a poor gift, the sister soon returned her. Finally he, in his own words, "set her adrift to care for herself." Here was this new Christian, holding on to the mother and turning out her helpless child to starve and die!

Thomas Auld and I disagreed in many ways. He found me unsuitable for his purpose. My city life, he said, had ruined me. One of my greatest faults was that I let his horse run away, and go down to his father-in-law's farm, about five miles away. I would then have to go after it. My reason for this "carelessness" was that I could always get something to eat when I went there. Master William Hamilton, my master's father-in-law, always gave his slaves enough to eat. I never left there hungry.

Thomas Auld finally said that he would stand my behavior no longer. I had lived with him for nine months, during which he had whipped me often. And so he said he would put me out to be "broken," and for this purpose, he hired me out for one year to a man named Edward Covey.

Covey was a poor man who rented the land he worked, as well as the slaves with which he worked it. Covey had a very high reputation for breaking young slaves, and this reputation was of great value to him. It allowed him to get his farm worked cheaply. Slaveholders were willing to lend their slaves to Covey for the sake of the training which they would receive. Covey was a pious man, a member and leader in the Methodist church. This added weight to his reputation as a "nigger-breaker." I knew all this, having been told of it by a young man who had lived there. Still I made the change gladly, for I was sure of getting enough to eat, which is not the smallest consideration to a hungry man.

# ✱ CHAPTER 10

I left Thomas Auld's house and went to live with Covey on January 1, 1833. I was now, for the first time in my life, a field hand. I found myself even more awkward than a country boy in a large city. I had been at my new home only a week before Covey gave me a very severe whipping, cutting my back, causing the blood to run, and raising ridges as large as my little finger on my flesh. This is what happened:

Covey sent me, very early in the morning on one of our coldest January days, to get a load of wood. He gave me a team of unbroken oxen. He had tied the end of a large rope around the horns of one of the oxen, and gave me the other end, and told me that if the ox started to run, that I must hold on.

I had never driven oxen before, and of course I was very awkward. I succeeded in getting to the edge of the woods without difficulty, but I had gotten only a little timber into the cart when the oxen became frightened by something. They started running, carrying the cart against trees and over stumps, in the most terrifying way. I expected every moment that my brains would be dashed out against the trees. After running like this for a good distance, they finally upset the cart against a tree.

How I escaped death, I do not know. There I was, entirely alone, in a thick wood which was strange to me. My cart was turned over and damaged, my oxen were tangled among the trees, and there was no one to help me. After a long time, I succeeded in getting my cart upright and the oxen disentangled and harnessed to the cart. I went back to the place where I had been chopping wood, and loaded my cart pretty heavily, thinking this might help tame the oxen. I then started home, having used up half the day.

I got out of the woods safely, and thought I was out of danger. I stopped my oxen to open the gate, and just as I did so, before I could catch hold of the rope, the oxen again started rushing through the gate, catching it between the wheel and the body of the cart, tearing it to pieces, and coming within a few inches of crushing me to death. And so twice in one short day, I escaped death by the merest chance.

On my return, I told Covey what had happened. He ordered me to return to the woods. I did so, with him following me there. Then he said that he would teach me not to waste his time and break gates. He went to a large gum tree and with his axe cut three large switches. After trimming them neatly with his pocketknife, he ordered me to take off my clothes. I did not answer, but stood with my clothes on. He repeated his order. I still said nothing, nor did I strip myself. At this he rushed at me with the fierceness of a tiger. He tore off my clothes, and whipped me until he had worn out his switches, cutting me so savagely that marks were visible for a long time. This whipping was the first of many just like it, and for similar offenses.

I lived with Covey one year. During the first six months, scarcely a week passed without his whipping me. I was seldom free from a sore back.

We were worked to the point of collapse. Long before sunup we were up, our horses fed, and by the first daylight we were in the field with our hoes and plowing teams. Covey gave us enough to eat, but scarcely time to eat it. We often had less than five minutes to take our meals. We were generally in the field until twilight. At certain times of year, midnight found us there as well.

Covey would be there with us. The way he did it was this. He would spend most of his afternoons asleep in bed. He would then come out fresh in the evening, ready to urge us on with his word, example, and frequently, his whip. Covey was one of the few slaveholders who could and did work with his hands. He was a hard-working man. He knew just what a man or boy could do. There was no deceiving him. Work went on in his absence almost as well as in his presence, and he had the trick of making us feel that he was always nearby. This he did by surprising us. He seldom approached us openly, if he could do it secretly. He was so cunning that we used to call him "the snake" among ourselves. When we were at work in the cornfield, he would sometimes crawl on his hands and knees, then all at once rise nearly in our midst, screaming out "Come on, faster!"

This being his mode of attack, it was never safe to stop a single minute. He came like a thief in the night. He was under every tree, behind every stump, in every bush, and at every window on the plantation. He would sometimes mount his horse, as if he were going to make the seven-mile trip to St. Michael's, and in half an hour you would see him coiled up in the corner of the wood fence, watching every move of the slaves. Again, he would sometimes walk up to us, and give us orders as though he was about to start on a long journey. But instead of leaving, he would turn back unseen and hide behind a tree, to watch us until the sun went down.

Covey's great talent was his power to deceive. His life was devoted to planning these deceptions. He even seemed to think he could deceive Almighty God. He would make a short prayer in the morning, and a long prayer at night, and few men seemed more religious than he. His family devotions always began with singing, and as he was a poor singer himself, the duty of starting the hymn generally fell on me. He would announce the hymn and nod at me to begin it. Sometimes I would do so; other times I would not. My lack of cooperation always confused him. To show that he didn't need my help, he would start singing and stagger through the hymn in the most awful manner. In this state of mind, he prayed with more spirit than ever.

Poor man! I truly believe that he actually deceived himself into believing he was a sincere worshipper of God. This, at the time when he was guilty of forcing his woman slave to commit adultery! The facts are this: Covey was a poor man. He was just getting started in life, and was able to buy just one slave. As shocking as it is, he bought her (in his words) as "a breeder." This woman was named Caroline. She was a large, able-bodied woman, about twenty years old. She had already given birth to one child, which proved her to be just what he wanted. After buying her, he hired a slave who was a married man to live with him for one year, and he used to lock them up together every night. The result was that, at the end of the year, the miserable woman gave birth to twins. Covey seemed highly pleased. He and his wife were so happy that while Caroline was recovering from the childbirth, nothing was too good for her. The children were quite an addition to his wealth.

The bitterest time of my slavery occurred during the first six months I lived with Covey. We worked in all weather. It was never too hot or too cold; it could never rain, blow, hail, or snow too hard for us to work in the fields. The longest days were too short for Covey, and the shortest nights too long for him. I was somewhat unmanageable when I first went there, but a few months of this discipline tamed me. Covey succeeded in breaking me.

I was broken in body, soul, and spirit. My natural resilience was crushed, my intellect weakened, my desire to read vanished, the cheerful spark in my eye died away. The dark night of slavery closed in upon me, and I was transformed from a man to a brute.

Sunday was my only leisure time. I spend this in sort of a trance, between sleep and waking, under a large tree. At times I would rise up, a flash of energy darting through my soul, accompanied by a beam of hope that flickered for a moment, then vanished. I sank down again, mourning my wretched condition. I was tempted to take my own life, and that of Covey, but was prevented by a combination of hope and fear. My sufferings on this plantation seem now more like a dream than reality.

Our house stood very close to the Chesapeake Bay, whose waters were white with sails from every corner of the globe. These beautiful ships, so delightful to the eyes of free men, tormented me. I have often, on a Sunday afternoon, stood alone on the banks of the bay and watched the countless sails moving off to the mighty ocean. There, with no one to hear me but God, I would pour out my thoughts:

"You are loose from your moorings, and are free! I am chained, a slave! You are freedom's swift-winged angels, while I am confined by bands of iron. Oh, if only I were free! If I were on one of your decks! Why was I born a man, to be made into a brute? Oh, God, save and deliver me! Let me be free. Is there a God? Why am I a slave? I will run away. I will not stand it. I will get caught, or get away. I have only one life to lose, and I had might as well lose it running as standing. Only think of it—just one hundred miles straight north, and I am free! God help me, I will try. I will take to the water. I saw the steamboats head northeast from North Point. I will do the same, and when I get to the head of the bay, I will turn my canoe loose and walk straight through Delaware into Pennsylvania. At the first chance, I will be off. Meanwhile, I will bear up best I can. I am not the only slave in the world. I can bear as much as any of them. Besides, I am only a boy, and all boys work for someone. Maybe my misery in slavery will only increase my happiness in freedom. There is a better day coming."

# ★ ★ ★ ★
## ★ CHAPTER 11
### ★ ★ ★ ★

$Y$ou have seen how a man was made into a slave. Now you will see how a slave was made into a man.

On one of the hottest days of August 1833, Bill Smith, William Hughes, a slave named Eli, and I were fanning wheat. I was carrying wheat to the fan, Bill was feeding it into the fan, Eli was turning the fan, and William was clearing away the fanned wheat. The work was simple but, to someone unused to it, exhausting.

At about three o'clock, I broke down. My strength failed me. I developed a violent headache and dizziness; I trembled in every limb. I stood as long as I could, continuing to stagger with my load to the hopper. When I could stand no longer, I fell, feeling as if I was held down by some immense weight. The fan, of course, stopped. Everyone had his own work to do, and the job could not continue if any one of us were absent.

Covey was at the house, about one hundred yards from where we were fanning. When he heard the fan stop, he rushed to the spot where we were. Bill explained that I was sick, and that there was no one to bring the wheat to the fan. I had by this time crawled into a shady spot, hoping to find relief by getting out of the sun.

Covey came to me and asked what was the matter. I told him as well as I could, for I had hardly enough strength to speak. He then gave me a savage kick in the side and told me to get up. I tried to do so, but fell back again. He kicked me again, ordering me to rise. I tried again, and managed to get to my feet, but as I stooped to get the tub I used to carry the wheat, I again staggered and fell. At this, Covey took up a hickory stick and struck me heavily on the head, making a large wound from which the blood flowed freely. Again, he told me to get up. I did not try to rise, having made up my mind to let him do his worst. Covey turned and left me lying there.

At this moment I decided to go to Thomas Auld, enter a complaint, and ask for his protection. In order to do this, I had to walk seven miles. Under the circumstances this was very nearly impossible. I was very weak, as much from the kicks and blows that I had received as by the severe fit of sickness I had experienced. But I watched for my chance, and while Covey was looking another way, I started for St. Michael's.

I managed to get a good ways toward the woods when Covey noticed me and shouted after me, threatening what he would do if I did not return. I ignored him and reached the woods as quickly as I could. Thinking he would surely catch up with me on the road, I continued to travel through the woods, keeping far enough from the road to avoid detection, but close enough to prevent losing my way.

I had gone only a little ways before my strength again failed. I fell down and lay there for some time. The blood was still oozing from the wound on my head. I thought I would bleed to death, but my hair became so matted with blood that it eventually stopped the flow. After lying there about forty-five minutes, I forced myself up again and walked on, through bogs and briers, tearing my bare feet at nearly every step. It took me about five hours to travel the seven miles, but eventually I arrived at Thomas Auld's store.

I must have been a sight to touch anyone who did not have a heart of iron. From the crown of my head to my feet, I was covered with blood. My hair was clotted with it; my shirt was stiff with it. My legs and feet were torn by thorns, and they too were covered with blood. I suppose I looked like a man who had escaped from a den of wild beasts.

In this state, I appeared before my master, begging him to use his authority to protect me. I told him what had happened as well as I could, and the story seemed, at times, to move him. He paced about as he talked, trying to justify Covey by saying he expected I deserved my beating. He asked me what I wanted. I told him I wanted a new home, for that if I lived with Covey again, that he would surely kill me.

Thomas Auld ridiculed the idea that there was any such danger. He said that he knew Covey; that he was a good man and that he could not think of taking me from him. He pointed out that he would lose a whole year's wages if I did not return; that I belonged to Covey for a year, and that I must go back to him. He added that I must not trouble him with any more stories, or that he himself would deal with me.

After so threatening me, he gave me a dose of medicine, telling me that I could stay in St. Michael's that night (it was quite late by then), but that I must go back to Covey's early in the morning. He added that he would whip me if I did not comply. I remained all night and, according to his orders, started off to Covey's in the morning, weary in body and broken in spirit. I had had no supper that night, nor breakfast in the morning.

I reached Covey's at about nine o'clock, and just as I was climbing over the fence that divided the neighbor's fields from ours, out ran Covey with his whip. Before he could reach me, I succeeded in getting to the cornfield, where I hid in the tall corn. He seemed very angry, and searched for me for a long time. He finally gave up, thinking (I suppose) that I would eventually get hungry and come out.

I spent most of that day in the woods. My alternatives were to go home and be whipped to death, or stay in the woods and starve to death. That night I encountered Sandy Jenkins, a slave that I knew a little. Sandy had a free wife who lived about four miles from Covey's. It being Saturday, he was on his way to see her, and very kindly invited me to go home with him. I went with him, talking the whole matter over.

I found Sandy to be a fine adviser, in his way. He told me very solemnly that I must go back to Covey, but that before I went, I must go with him into another part of the woods to dig up a certain root. I must take some of it with me, carrying it always on my right side, and it would make it impossible for Covey or any other white man to whip me. He said he had carried this root for years, and he had never been struck in all that time.

I at first rejected the idea, not believing that a root could have any such power, but Sandy pleaded with me, telling me at least it could do me no harm. To please him, I finally took the root, and according to his instruction, carried it on my right side.

This was Sunday morning. I started for home, and as I entered the gate, out came Covey on his way to church. He spoke to me very kindly, told me to drive the pigs away from a nearby lot, and passed me by. Now, this odd conduct made me wonder if there was something in the root that Sandy had given me. If it had been any day but Sunday, I could have thought of no other explanation for Covey's conduct.

All went well until Monday morning. Then the power of the root was fully tested. Long before daylight, I was called to go rub, curry, and feed the horses. I was glad to obey. But while I was busy in the stable, throwing down hay from the loft, Covey walked in carrying a long rope. He leapt at me, seizing my legs, and began to tie me up. As I realized what he was up to, I sprang up and, as he was still holding my legs, sprawled to the floor.

Covey seemed to think he had me, and could do what he pleased. But at this moment—from where the spirit came, I do not know—I resolved to fight. I seized Covey hard by the throat and stood up. He held on to me and I to him. My resistance was so unexpected that Covey seemed taken aback. This gave me courage. Covey called out to Hughes for help. Hughes came, and while Covey held me, he tried to tie my hands. While Hughes was busy with the rope, I gave him a heavy kick under the ribs.

The kick not only weakened Hughes, but Covey as well. When he saw Hughes doubled over with pain, his courage failed. He asked me if I would keep resisting. I said I would; that he had used me like a brute for six months, and that I would take it no longer. With that, he tried to drag me to a stick that was lying outside the stable door. But as he was leaning over to get the stick, I seized him with both hands by his collar, and threw him to the ground.

By this time, Bill had run in, hearing Covey's cries for help. Covey shouted, "Take hold of him, take hold of him!" But Bill said that his master had hired him out to work, not to help whip me, and he left.

Covey and I fought for nearly two hours. Finally, panting and gasping, he let me go, saying that if I had not resisted, he would not have whipped me so much. Actually he hadn't whipped me at all. He had not drawn blood from me; I had drawn blood from *him*.

The whole six months after that, that I spent with Covey, he never laid a finger upon me. He would occasionally say that he didn't want to have to whip me again. "No," I thought, "you don't want to, for you will come out of it worse than you did before."

From this time on, I was never again what you might call whipped, though I remained a slave four more years. I had several fights, but was never whipped.

It surprised me for a long time that Covey did not have me taken by the police to the whipping-post, to be punished for the crime of raising my hand against a white man. The only explanation I can think of is this: Covey enjoyed a reputation as a first-rate overseer and negro-breaker. That reputation was of great importance to him. If he had sent me— a boy of sixteen—to the public whipping-post, his reputation would have been lost.

My term of service to Covey ended on Christmas Day, 1833. The days between Christmas and New Year's Day were the slaves' holiday; we were not required to do any work beyond taking care of the farm animals. Those of us who had families a distance away were generally allowed to spend the week with them. Otherwise, the holiday was spent in various ways. The thinking and industrious ones employed themselves making brooms, mats, horse collars, and baskets. Others hunted possums, rabbits, and raccoons. But by far, the greatest number of us engaged in sports and recreation such as ball-playing, wrestling, running races, fiddling, dancing, and drinking whiskey.

This last activity was by far the most pleasing to our masters. In the master's eyes, a slave who worked during the holidays hardly deserved them. Such a slave was seen as one who rejected his master's gracious favor. It was thought a disgrace not to get drunk at Christmas.

From what I saw of the effect of these holidays, I believe them to be among the slaveholders' most effective ways of keeping down any spirit of rebellion. They served as safety valves to carry off the rebellious spirit of enslaved humanity. They are, in my opinion, part of the gross fraud and inhumanity of slavery. They are supposedly a generous custom, but in fact they are born of the grossest selfishness. The slaveholders love to see the slaves spending those days in a manner that makes the slaves as glad of their ending as of their beginning. The point seems to be to disgust the slaves with freedom, by plunging them into the lowest depths of immorality and self-indulgence.

For instance, the slaveholder not only likes to see the slave drink of his own accord, but will go to great lengths to make his slaves drunk. One way is to make bets as to which slave can drink the most without getting drunk. In this way they make the whole multitude drink to excess. So, when the holidays ended, we staggered up from the filth of our wallowing, took a long breath, and marched to the field—feeling, on the whole, glad to leave what our master had told us was "freedom" and enter back into the arms of slavery.

I have said that this mode of treatment is part of the whole system of fraud and inhumanity of slavery. It is true. The idea is to disgust the slave with freedom, by allowing him to see only the abuse of it. This principle is carried out in other ways as well. For instance, a slave loves molasses; he steals some. His master goes off to town and buys a large quantity. He returns, takes his whip, and commands the slave to eat the molasses until the poor fellow is sick at the very thought of it. The same technique is sometimes used to make slaves refrain from asking for more food than their regular allowance. A slave runs through his allowance and asks for more. His enraged master gives him a large amount, and insists that he eat it within a given time. Then, if the slave complains that he cannot eat it, he is said to be impossible to satisfy and is whipped for being hard to please!

# CHAPTER 12

On the first of January, 1834, I left Covey, and went to live with William Freeland, who lived about three miles from St. Michael's. I found Freeland a very different man from Covey. Though not rich, he was what would be called an educated southern gentleman. He was a slaveholder, but he seemed to possess some regard for honor, some reverence for justice, and some respect for humanity.

Another advantage of working for Freeland was that he did not claim to be religious. I state most strongly that the religion of the south is a mere cover for the most horrid crimes. It justifies the most appalling barbarity, and it shelters the darkest, foulest, most infernal deeds of slaveholders. If I were put again into the chains of slavery, I would regard being the slave of a religious man the greatest calamity that could befall me. For of all the slaveholders with whom I have ever met, religious slaveholders are the worst. They are the meanest and basest, the most cruel and cowardly of all.

Freeland's neighbors included two ministers in the Reformed Methodist church: Daniel Weeden and Rigby Hopkins. Weeden owned, among other slaves, a woman whose back he kept raw for weeks at a time from whippings. His rule was this: whether or not a slave misbehaves, their master should whip them occasionally to remind them of his authority. Hopkins was even worse than Weeden. He often boasted of his ability to manage slaves. Every Monday morning he had at least one of his slaves whipped. He did this not only to torture those who were whipped but also to strike terror into those who were not. His idea was to whip for the smallest offenses, to prevent larger ones.

It would astonish you, if you are unaccustomed to the slaveholding life, to see how easily a slaveholder could find reason to punish. A mere look, word, or motion—a mistake, accident, or lack of power—are all matters for which a slave may be whipped at any time. Does a slave look dissatisfied? Then he has the devil in him, and it must be whipped out. Does he speak loudly when spoken to by his master? Then he is getting high-minded and should be taken down. Does he forget to take off his hat at the approach of a white person? Then he is lacking respect and should be whipped. Does he ever dare to defend his actions when punished for them? Then he is guilty of impudence—one of the greatest crimes of which a slave can be guilty. Does he suggest a different way of doing things from that ordered by his master? He is getting above himself, and nothing less than a beating will do. Does he, while plowing, break a plow? Or while hoeing, break a hoe? It is due to his carelessness, and for it he must be whipped.

Hopkins would always find something of this sort to justify the use of the lash. Slaves would rather live with any man in the whole county than with him. And yet there was not a man anywhere around who made such noisy claims of religion, or was more active in revival meetings, more attentive to his church, more involved in prayer and preaching meetings—no one who prayed earlier, later, louder, and longer, than this reverend slave driver.

But I must return to Freeland and to my experience while in his employment. He, like Covey, gave us enough to eat; unlike Covey, he also gave us sufficient time to take our meals. He worked us hard, but only between sunrise and sunset. He required a good deal of work to be done, but gave us good tools with which to work. His farm was large, but he employed hands enough to work it. My treatment, while in his employment, was heavenly compared with what I experienced at the hands of Covey.

Freeland himself owned only two slaves, Henry Harris and John Harris. The rest of his workers were hired hands. These consisted of myself, Sandy Jenkins (the same man who had given me the root), and Handy Caldwell. Henry and John were quite intelligent, and soon after I went there, I created in them a strong desire to learn how to read. This desire spread to the others also. They came up with some old spelling books, and begged me to start a school on Sundays.

From then on, I devoted my Sundays to teaching my beloved fellow slaves how to read. None of them knew their letters when I went there. Some of the slaves of the neighboring farms heard what was going on, and also took advantage of this little opportunity to learn to read. It was understood by all that we must keep our Sunday school a quiet matter. We did not tell our religious masters that, instead of spending the Sabbath wrestling, boxing, and drinking whisky, we were trying to learn how to read. They would much rather see us engaged in those degrading sports, than to see us behaving like intellectual, moral, and accountable beings. My blood boils as I think of the manner in which those upright church leaders rushed in upon us with sticks and stones, and broke up our little Sabbath school at St. Michael's—all calling themselves Christians! Humble followers of the Lord Jesus Christ! But I am again getting off my topic.

I held my Sabbath school at the house of a free colored man, whose name I dare not mention here even though the crime of holding the school was committed ten years ago. At one time I had over forty scholars, and scholars of the best sort—those who greatly wanted to learn. They were of all ages, though mostly adult men and women. I look back to those Sundays with more pleasure than I can say. They were great days to my soul. The work of instructing my dear fellow slaves was the sweetest with which I have ever been blessed. We loved each other, and to leave them at the end of the Sabbath was difficult indeed.

When I think that these precious souls are still today shut up in the prison-house of slavery, my feelings overcome me. I am almost ready to ask, "Does a righteous God govern the universe? Why does he hold the thunder in his right hand, if not to strike down the oppressor?" These dear souls did not come to Sabbath school because it was popular to do so. I did not teach them because doing so improved my reputation. They knew that every moment they spent in that school, they were at risk of being snatched up and given thirty-nine lashes. They came because they wished to learn. Their minds had been starved by their cruel masters. They had been shut up in mental darkness. I taught them because it was the delight of my soul to do something that could better the condition of my race.

I kept up my school nearly the whole year I lived with Freeland. Besides my Sabbath school, I spent three evenings in the week during the winter, teaching the slaves at home. I have the happiness of knowing that several of those who came to Sabbath school learned how to read, and that one, at least, is now free through my efforts.

The year passed smoothly. It seemed only about half as long as the year which preceded it. I went through it without receiving a single blow. I will give Freeland credit for being the best master I ever had, until I became my own master. But the ease of that year was mostly owing to friendship of my fellow slaves. They were noble souls. They not only possessed loving hearts, but brave ones. I loved them with a love stronger than any I have experienced since.

It is sometimes said that we slaves do not love and confide in each other. I can answer truly that I never loved or confided in any people more than my fellow slaves, and especially those with whom I lived at Freeland's. I believe we would have died for each other. We never made decisions about important matters without discussion with one another. We never moved separately. We were one, both due to our natural friendship and to the mutual hardships we experienced.

# CHAPTER 13

At the close of the year 1834, Freeland again hired me from Thomas Auld to work through the year 1835. But, by this time, I began to want to live upon free land as well as with Freeland. I was no longer content to live with him or any other slaveholder. I began to prepare myself for a final struggle, which should decide my fate one way or the other. I was nearly a grown man; year after year had passed, and I was still a slave. These thoughts burned within me—I knew I must do something. I therefore resolved that 1835 should not pass without my making an attempt to become free.

But I was not willing to cherish this determination alone. My fellow slaves were dear to me. I wanted them to share with me this life-giving hope. I therefore, though very carefully, began to determine their views and feelings in regard to their condition, and to plant in their minds thoughts of freedom. I thought of ways we might escape and, meanwhile, worked whenever I could to convince them of the fraud and inhumanity of slavery.

I went first to Henry, next to John, then to the others. I found in them all warm hearts and noble spirits. They were ready to hear, and ready to act when a practical plan should be proposed. This was what I wanted. I talked to them about how slavery robbed us of our manhood if we gave in to our enslavement without at least one effort to be free. We met often, and talked frequently, and shared our hopes and fears, and described the difficulties, real and imagined, which we might meet.

At times we were tempted to give up and try to be content with our wretched lives; at others, we were firm and unbending in our determination to go. Whenever we suggested any plan, there was hesitation—the odds against us were fearful. Our path was littered with great obstacles. And, if we succeeded in escaping, our right to be free was still in question. We could be seized and returned to slavery. We could see no spot this side of the ocean where we could be free. We knew nothing about Canada. Our knowledge of the north did not extend farther than New York, and it was horrible to imagine reaching there and being harassed forever with the prospect of being returned to slavery.

On the one hand, we saw slavery: a stern reality, but one that we knew. On the other hand, back in the dim distance, stood a doubtful freedom, beckoning us to come and share its hospitality. When we let ourselves imagine the road that stood between us and that freedom, we were frequently horrified. We saw ourselves being overtaken and torn to pieces by the fangs of the terrible blood-hound. We were stung by scorpions, chased by wild beasts, bitten by snakes, and finally, after having nearly reached the desired spot— after swimming rivers, encountering wild animals, sleeping in the woods, suffering hunger and nakedness—we were caught by our pursuers, and, when we resisted, shot dead upon the spot! As I say, this picture sometimes terrified us, and made us think it might be better to put up with the evil we knew than run to an evil we did not.

In coming to a firm decision to run away, we did more than Patrick Henry when he said, "Give me liberty or give me death." With us it was a doubtful liberty at most, and almost certain death if we failed. But for my part, I preferred death to hopeless bondage.

One of us, Sandy, gave up the idea of running away, but still encouraged us. Our group then consisted of Henry Harris, John Harris, Henry Bailey, Charles Roberts, and myself. Henry Bailey was my uncle and belonged to Thomas Auld. Charles had married my aunt; he belonged to my master's father-in-law, William Hamilton.

The plan we finally decided on was this: We would get a large canoe belonging to Hamilton, and on the Saturday night before Easter, paddle directly up the Chesapeake Bay. When we reached the head of the bay, seventy or eighty miles from where we lived, we planned to abandon the canoe. We would then walk, following the guidance of the North Star, until we got beyond the limits of Maryland.

Traveling by water, we reasoned, we would look less like runaways than like fishermen. If we should travel by land, we would be questioned every step of the way. Anyone having a white face could stop us and demand that we explain ourselves.

The week before our intended start, I wrote several documents, one for each of us. As well as I can remember, they read like this: "This is to certify that I, the undersigned, have given the bearer, my servant, full liberty to go to Baltimore to spend the Easter holidays. Written with my own hand this day in

1835. William Hamilton, near St. Michael's, Talbot County, Maryland."

We were not going to Baltimore, but in going up the bay, we went toward Baltimore.

As the time approached for our departure, our anxiety became more and more intense. It was truly a matter of life and death for us. At this time, I was very active in explaining every difficulty, removing every doubt, and calming every fear. I assured my friends that the battle was half won the instant we made the move. We had talked long enough; we were now ready for action. If we were not ready now, we never would be; and if we did not move now, we might as well sit down and admit we were only fit to be slaves. And this, none of us were prepared to acknowledge.

Every man stood firm. At our last meeting, we pledged in the most solemn manner, that at the appointed time, we would certainly start in pursuit of freedom. This was in the middle of the week, and we were to leave Saturday night. We went, as usual, to our different workplaces, our minds reeling with thoughts of our hazardous undertaking. We tried to conceal our feelings as much us possible, and I think we succeeded very well.

After a painful waiting, Saturday morning came. I greeted it with joy, no matter what sadness it might bring. Friday night had been a sleepless one for me. I probably felt more anxious than the rest, because I was considered the leader of the whole affair. The responsibility of success or failure lay heavily upon me.

The first two hours of that morning were such as I never experienced before and hope never to again. Early in the morning, we went as usual to the field. We were spreading manure. All at once, as I worked, I was overwhelmed with an indescribable feeling. I turned to Sandy, who was nearby, and said, "We are betrayed!"

"I just had the same thought," he said.

We said no more. I was never more certain of anything.

The horn was blown as usual, and we went up to the house for breakfast. Just as I got to the house, I saw four white men and two colored men in the lane. The white men were on horseback, and the colored ones were walking behind, as if tied. I watched them a few moments until they reached our lane gate. Here they stopped, and tied the colored men to the gatepost.

In a few moments, in rode Hamilton looking highly excited. He asked if Freeland was in, and rode up to the barn with extraordinary speed to find him. In a few moments, he and Freeland returned to the house. By this time, the three local police officers arrived. After talking a while, they all walked up to the kitchen door. There was no one in the kitchen but myself and John. Henry and Sandy were up at the barn.

Freeland called me, saying there were some gentlemen at the door who wished to see me. I stepped to the door and asked what they wanted. They instantly seized me, tying my hands. I insisted upon knowing what the matter was. They finally said that they had learned I had been in a "scrape," and that I was to be questioned before my master. If their information proved false, they said, I should not be hurt.

In a few moments, they succeeded in tying John. They then turned to Henry, who had by this time returned, and commanded him to cross his hands. "I won't!" said Henry, in a firm tone.

"Won't you?" one law officer said.

"No, I won't!" said Henry, in a still stronger tone.

With this, two of the officers pulled out their shining pistols and swore that they would make him cross his hands or kill him. Each cocked his pistol. With fingers on the trigger, they walked up to Henry, saying that if he did not cross his hands, they would blow his damned heart out.

"Shoot me, shoot me!" said Henry. "You can't kill me but once. Shoot, shoot—and be damned! I won't be tied!" This he said in a tone of loud defiance. At the same time, with a motion as quick as lightning, he struck the pistols from the hand of each officer.

The officers fell upon him, and, after beating him, they finally overpowered him and got him tied.

During the scuffle, I managed to get my forged pass out and put it in the fire. We were all now tied; and just as we were to leave for Easton jail, Freeland's mother came to the door with her hands full of biscuits. She divided them between Henry and John, and then spoke to me saying, "You devil! You yellow devil! It was you that put it into the heads of Henry and John to run away. If it wasn't for you, you long-legged mulatto devil, Henry and John would never have thought of such a thing."

I did not answer and was immediately hurried off toward St. Michael's.

A moment before the scuffle with Henry, Hamilton had suggested that we be searched for the forged papers he understood I had written. But just before that search could take place, his help was needed in helping to tie

Henry. In the excitement of the next few moments they either forgot to search us or decided it was unsafe to do so. So as yet, they had no proof against us.

When we got about half way to St. Michael's, Henry managed to quietly ask me what he should do with his pass. I told him to eat it with his biscuit and to admit to nothing. We passed the word around: "Admit nothing!"

Our confidence in each other was unshaken. We had decided to succeed or fail together, and after this calamity we felt the same. We were now prepared for anything.

When we reached St. Michael's, we underwent a sort of examination. We all denied that we ever intended to run away. We did this more to bring out the evidence against us than from any hope of being believed. We learned that the evidence against us came from one person. Our master would not tell who it was, but we felt certain that we knew.

We were sent off to the jail at Easton, where we were put into the sheriff's hands. Henry, John, and I were placed in one room together, and Charles and Henry Bailey in another.

We had been in jail scarcely twenty minutes, when a swarm of slave traders flocked in to look at us. Such a set of beings I never saw before! I felt I was surrounded by so many fiends from hell. They laughed and grinned at us saying, "Ah, my boys! We have got you, haven't we?" After taunting us, they began to examine us, trying to determine our value. They rudely laughed at us, asking if we would not like to have them for our masters. We would not answer them. Then they cursed and swore at us, telling us that they could take the devil out of us in a very little while, if we were only in their hands.

Jail was more comfortable than we expected. We did not get much to eat, nor was the food very good, but we had a good clean room, and we could see out the windows into the street. Upon the whole, we got along very well, so far as the jail and its keeper were concerned.

Immediately after Easter, to our surprise, Hamilton and Freeland came up to Easton and took Charles, the two Henrys, and John, out of jail and went home with them, leaving me alone. This separation caused me more pain than anything else in the whole episode. I suppose that Hamilton and Freeland had talked together and had decided that as I was the ringleader, they would take the others home and sell me, as a warning to those that remained.

I was now left to my fate. I was all alone and within the walls of a stone prison. Only a few days before, I was full of hope. I expected to have been safe in a land of freedom, but now I was sunk down to the utmost despair. I thought the possibility of freedom was gone. I was kept in this way about one week. But at the end of that time, to my utter astonishment, Thomas Auld arrived and took me out. He intended to send me to Alabama with a gentleman he knew. But, for some reason, he did not send me to Alabama. He decided instead to send me back to Baltimore, to live again with his brother Hugh, and to learn a trade. Thus, after an absence of three years and one month, I once more returned to my old home in Baltimore.

# CHAPTER 14

Hugh Auld hired me out to Mr. William Gardner, a shipbuilder, on Fell's Point. I was put there to learn how to caulk—in other words, to seal up the seams between a ship's timbers. However, it proved a very bad time and place for me to learn this trade.

Gardner was engaged that spring in building two large man-of-war brigs for the Mexican government. The vessels were to be launched in July of that year. If he missed that deadline, Gardner would lose a considerable sum of money, and so when I arrived, all was hurry. There was no time to learn anything. Every man had to do that which he knew how to do.

When I entered the shipyard, my orders from Gardner were to do whatever the carpenters commanded. This meant I was at the beck and call of about seventy-five men. They were all my masters; their word was to be my law. My situation was most difficult. At times I needed a dozen pair of hands. Three or four voices would strike my ear at the same moment.

It was, "Fred, come help me here. Fred, come carry this timber yonder. Fred, bring that roller here. Fred, go get a fresh can of water. Fred, come help saw off the end of this timber. Fred, go quick, and get the crowbar. Fred, go to the blacksmith's shop, and get a new punch. Hurry, Fred! Run and bring me a cold chisel. Hey, nigger! Come, turn this grindstone. Blast you, darky, why don't you heat up some pitch? Come here! Go there! Hold on where you are! Damn you, if you move, I'll knock your brains out!"

Gardner's shipyard was my school for eight months. I might have remained there longer except for a terrible fight I had with four of the white apprentices, in which my left eye was nearly knocked out. This was how it happened.

Until soon after I went there, white and black shipcarpenters worked side by side, and no one seemed to have any problem with that. Many of the black carpenters were freemen. Things seemed to be going on very well. But all at once, the white carpenters laid down their tools, and said they would not work with free colored workmen. Their reason, they said, was that if free colored carpenters were encouraged, they would soon take the trade into their own hands, and poor white men would be thrown out of employment. Taking advantage of Gardner's need for fast progress, they broke off, swearing they would work no longer unless he fires the black carpenters.

Now, though I was not a free carpenter, the white carpenters' talk did have its effect on me. My fellow apprentices began to feel it was degrading to work with me. They began to put on airs, talked about the "niggers" taking over the country, and said we all ought to be killed. Encouraged by the carpenters, they made my condition as hard as they could, tormenting me constantly and sometimes striking me. I, of course, kept the vow I made after the fight with Covey, and struck back, regardless of the consequences.

As long as I could fight them separately, I did very well, for I could whip any of them. However, they eventually joined forces, and came upon me armed with sticks, stones, and heavy handspikes. One came in front with a half brick. There was one at each side of me, and one behind me. The one behind me ran up with a spike and struck me a heavy blow upon the head. It stunned me; I fell, and they were all on me at once, beating me with their fists. I gathered my strength and rose to my hands and knees, but just then one of them wearing heavy boots gave me a powerful kick in the left eye. My eyeball seemed to have burst. When they saw my eye closed and badly swollen, they left me.

I seized the handspike and ran after them. But here the carpenters interfered, and I thought I might as well give it up. It was impossible to fight against so many.

All this took place in sight of no less than fifty white shipcarpenters, and not one tried to help. In fact, some cried, "Kill the damned nigger! Kill him! Kill him! He struck a white person." My only chance for life was in running. I managed to get away without further injury, but barely so, for to strike a white man is to invite death by lynching. That was the law in Gardner's shipyard, and in many places outside of Gardner's shipyard.

I went directly home and told Hugh Auld what had happened. He was far more sympathetic than his brother Thomas had been under similar circumstances. He listened carefully and expressed indignation. Enraged, he cursed those who had done the deed.

My puffy eye and blood-covered face moved Sophia Auld to tears. She sat down next to me, washed the blood from my face, and, with a mother's tenderness, bound my head, covering the wounded eye with a piece of fresh lean beef. Seeing her return to her old kind, affectionate ways almost made up for my suffering.

As soon as I recovered a bit, Hugh Auld took me to a lawyer named Watson to see what could be done. Watson asked who had witnessed the assault. Hugh Auld told him that it had occurred in Gardner's shipyard at midday, while many men were present. Watson said that he couldn't do anything unless some white man came forward and testified. My word was worth nothing. If I had been killed in the presence of a thousand blacks, their combined testimony would not have prompted the arrest of even one of the murderers.

Of course, it was impossible to get any white to testify on my behalf against other whites. Even those who may have sympathized with me wouldn't do this; it required more courage than they possessed. At that time the slightest show of humanity toward a black was condemned as abolitionism, and that was a dangerous word. Bloody-minded people were fond of saying, "Damn the abolitionists!" and "Damn the niggers!" Nothing was done about the assault. Such was, and such remains, the state of things in the Christian city of Baltimore.

Finding that he could get no satisfaction,

Hugh Auld refused to let me return to Gardner's shipyard. He kept me himself, and his wife cared for my wound until it healed.

Hugh Auld then took me to Walter Price's shipyard, where he was foreman. There I was taught to caulk. Within one year of my leaving Gardner's, I was able to earn wages equal to those of the most experienced caulkers. I sought my own jobs, made my own contracts, and collected the money that I earned—about $7.00 a week, sometimes as much as $9.00. The money was paid to me and rightfully was mine. Yet, each Saturday night, I handed over my earnings to Hugh Auld. Why? Because he could force me to.

Even so, my life was much smoother and more comfortable than before. When I couldn't get caulking work, I did nothing. During my leisure time, old thoughts of freedom stole over me. While in Gardner's employment, I had been under such constant pressure that I had thought of almost nothing but my survival. I almost had forgotten about liberty.

I have observed this about my slavery: improved conditions increased, rather than lessened, my desire to be free. To make slaves content, it is necessary to make them believe that slavery is right. This can be done only by preventing them from thinking.

# CHAPTER 15

I now come to the time in my life when I finally escaped from slavery. It would give me much pleasure to reveal all the facts connected with my escape, but that could create great difficulties for others. Instead I will state only those facts for which I alone am responsible and can be made to suffer.

In the early part of 1838, I became quite restless. I could see no reason why I should pour the rewards of my toil into Hugh Auld's purse at the end of every week. Whenever I brought Hugh Auld my weekly wages, he would count the money, then look me in the face with a robber-like fierceness and ask, "Is this all?" He was satisfied with nothing less than every cent. However, when I made $6.00, he sometimes gave me 6¢ to encourage me and, I believe, ease his conscience. To me, his giving me any part of my wages showed that he knew I was entitled to all of them.

My discontent grew. I constantly watched for a way to escape. Finding no direct way, I decided to try to save money for my escape. I asked Hugh Auld if I could work for myself. After some reflection, he agreed—provided that I would bear the expenses of my clothing and caulking tools, pay for room and board somewhere, and, at the end of each week, give him $3.00. Because my weekly expenses would include about $2.50 for room and board and about another 50¢ for clothing and tools, this meant that my weekly expenses would total about $6.00. Rain or shine, work or no work, at the end of each week I would have to give Hugh Auld $3.00. This arrangement would relieve him of all need to look after me while guaranteeing him $3.00 each week. In contrast, I would have increased responsibilities and anxieties. Still, I preferred this new arrangement to my old situation. To bear a freeman's responsibilities was a step toward freedom, and I was determined to succeed.

I dedicated myself to making money. I was ready to work day and night. By my industry I was able to meet my expenses and put aside a little money every week. I continued in this way from May to August.

Then, one Saturday evening, I went with some friends to a camp meeting about ten miles from Baltimore. Earlier in the week, I had agreed to go with them. I had planned to give Hugh Auld his weekly $3.00 before going; however, when the day arrived, I was delayed by my employer. Rather than disappoint my friends, I met them at the agreed time and went to the camp meeting without paying Hugh Auld. I knew that he had no immediate need for the money. I stayed at the camp meeting one day longer than I had intended, but I called on Hugh Auld as soon as I returned.

I found him very angry. He said that he had a great mind to give me a severe whipping. He asked how I dared to leave the city without his permission. I responded that I had not known that I needed to ask him where I could go and when. This reply troubled him. After reflecting a few moments, he said that I no longer could work for myself. He said that the next thing he knew, I would be running away. He told me to bring my tools and clothing home.

I did as he demanded, but instead of working, I spent the whole week doing nothing. I did this to get back at him.

Saturday night he asked me for my week's wages. I told him that I had none; I had done no work that week. We nearly came to blows.

He raved, swearing his determination to get hold of me. I said nothing, but I was determined that if he laid a hand on me, it would be blow for blow. He did not strike me but said that I should work continuously from now on.

The next day, I thought the matter over and decided that on the third of September I would make a second attempt to escape. I had three weeks to prepare for my journey.

Early on Monday, before Hugh Auld had time to arrange any job for me, I went out and got work at Mr. Butler's shipyard. At the end of the week, I brought Hugh Auld nearly $9.00. He seemed very pleased. My reason for working steadily was to remove any suspicion from his mind that I was planning to run away. I believe that he thought I never had been more content than at the very time that I was planning to escape. The second week passed, and again I brought him my full wages. He was so pleased that he gave me 25¢ and advised me to make good use of it. I told him that I would.

Outwardly things went smoothly, but inwardly I was troubled. I had a number of warmhearted friends in Baltimore—friends whom I loved. The thought of being separated from them forever was extremely painful. I believe that thousands more slaves would escape if it were not for the strong cords of affection that bind them to their friends. Besides the pain of separation, I dreaded failure. The failure of my first escape attempt tormented me. I felt certain that if I failed again, I would be severely punished and placed where I never could hope to escape.

But I remained firm. On September 3, 1838, I left my chains. I reached New York without any interruption. What direction I traveled, and by what mode of transportation, I must leave unsaid for the reasons that I have mentioned.

# CHAPTER 16

I frequently have been asked how I felt when I found myself in a free state. I never have been able to answer that question to my satisfaction. I felt the highest excitement that I ever have experienced. In writing to a dear friend immediately after my arrival in New York, I said that I felt like someone who had escaped a den of hungry lions.

However, this state of mind soon subsided. I still could be captured and taken back to slavery's tortures. This thought filled me with anxiety. Even worse was the great loneliness that overcame me. I was a stranger in the midst of thousands of people. I was afraid to speak to anyone: speaking to the wrong person might place me in the hands of money-loving kidnappers whose business it was to lie in wait for fugitive slaves. I adopted the motto "Trust no one." I saw an enemy in every white and a cause for distrust in nearly every black.

Thank heaven, I remained in this sad situation only a short time. I was relieved from it by David Ruggles, whose kindness I'll never forget. I am glad for this opportunity to express the love and gratitude that I feel toward him. David now is blind and in need of the same kindness that he generously showed to others. I had been in New York only a few days when he found me and kindly took me to his boarding house. He was deeply involved in the cases of a number of fugitive slaves. Though watched and hemmed in on almost every side, he was more than a match for his enemies.

Soon after I went to David, he asked me where I wanted to go. He believed that it was unsafe for me to stay in New York. I told him that I was a caulker and would like to go where I could get work. I thought of going to Canada, but he advised me to go to New Bedford, Massachusetts, thinking that I would be able to find work there.

At this time, Anna Murray, a freewoman who was my intended wife, came to New York. I had written to her immediately after my arrival, asking her to come. A few days after she arrived, we were married. After the wedding, with a gift of $5.00 from David, we boarded a steamboat bound for Newport, on our way to New Bedford.

When we arrived in New Bedford, we were directed to the house of Nathan Johnson. He and his wife were most kind and hospitable and took a lively interest in our welfare. They truly deserved the name of abolitionists. We now began to feel safe and started to prepare ourselves for the duties and responsibilities of a life of freedom.

At breakfast on our first morning in New Bedford, the Johnsons asked me what name I wanted to use. My mother had named me Frederick Augustus Washington Bailey. Long ago I had stopped using my two middle names, so I generally was known as Frederick Bailey. When I had reached New York, I had changed my name to Frederick Johnson. But there were so many Johnsons in New Bedford that I now preferred some other name. I gave Nathan the privilege of choosing a new surname for me. He had just been reading Sir Walter Scott's poem "The Lady of the Lake," so he suggested that I adopt the name of its hero: Douglass. From that time on, I have been called Frederick Douglass.

New Bedford's general appearance greatly surprised me. While a slave, I had formed a mistaken impression of living conditions in the North. I had supposed that Northerners possessed few of the comforts, and none of the luxuries, that slaveholders enjoy. Because Northerners owned no slaves, I had supposed that they lived like non-slaveholding white Southerners, who are exceedingly poor. I had expected Northerners to be rough, uneducated people living in harsh simplicity. On my first full day in New Bedford, I visited the wharves, where I witnessed the strongest proofs of wealth. There were many ships of the finest model, best condition, and largest size. I was walled in by massive warehouses, filled with every necessity and comfort. Almost everyone seemed to be working, but quietly—in contrast to the situation in Baltimore shipyards. I heard no loud songs from the men loading and unloading ships, no noisy oaths or curses from the workmen. I saw no whipping of men, yet all the work seemed to proceed smoothly. Every man appeared to understand his work and do it with a sober, cheerful determination that indicated a sense of his own dignity.

From the wharves I strolled around the town, gazing with wonder and admiration at the splendid churches, beautiful homes, and finely cultivated gardens. Everywhere was an amount of wealth, comfort, and refinement such as I never had seen in slaveholding

Maryland. Everything looked clean, new, and beautiful. I saw no dilapidated houses with poverty-stricken residents, no half-naked children and barefoot women such as I customarily had seen in Maryland. The people looked healthier, happier, and more able than any I ever had seen. For once, I could see extreme wealth without being saddened by seeing extreme poverty alongside it.

To me, however, the most astonishing and interesting thing was the condition of the blacks. Like me, many of them had escaped to New Bedford from slavery. I found many who had been free less than seven years but were living in finer houses and enjoying more of life's comforts than the average Maryland slaveholder. My friend Nathan Johnson lived in a neater house, dined at a better table, read more newspapers, and better understood the nation's moral, religious, and political character than nine-tenths of the slaveholders in Talbot County, Maryland. Yet Nathan was a working man. His hands were hardened by toil, as were those of his wife.

I found the blacks much more spirited than I had expected. They shared a determination to protect one another from bloodthirsty kidnappers. Soon after my arrival I heard a story that illustrated this spirit. A free black and a fugitive slave were on unfriendly terms. The freeman was heard threatening to tell the runaway's master where to find the fugitive. Immediately the black community called a meeting to discuss "business of importance." They invited the freeman. At the meeting the people appointed an old, religious gentleman as chairman. This gentleman offered a prayer and then said, "Friends, we have got him here. I recommend that you young men take him outside and kill him." A number of men bolted at the freeman, but others stopped them. The betrayer escaped and has not been seen in New Bedford since.

Three days after my arrival I found employment helping to load a ship with barrels of oil. It was new, dirty, and hard work for me, but I did it with a glad heart and willing hand. I was my own master. Only those who have been slaves can understand the joy that I felt. For the first time my earnings were my own. No Hugh Auld stood ready to rob me of them. I worked with a pleasure that I never had experienced before. I was working for myself and my new wife. A new existence had begun.

When I finished that job, I looked for work as a caulker. But there was prejudice among the white caulkers, and they refused to work with me. Unable to work at my trade, I prepared to do any kind of work that I could get. Nathan kindly lent me his saw and carpentry horse, and I soon had plenty of jobs. There was no work too dirty or hard. I was ready to saw wood, shovel coal, sweep chimneys, or roll oil barrels. I did all of this for nearly three years before I became known to the anti-slavery world.

About four months after I arrived in New Bedford, I started subscribing to the *Liberator*. I read this newspaper from week to week with deeper feelings than I can describe. It became my meat and drink; it set my soul on fire. Its sympathy for my fellow slaves, denunciations of slaveholders, exposures of slavery, and powerful attacks on slavery's defenders thrilled me. The *Liberator* introduced me to the principles, activities, and spirit of the anti-slavery movement. I took up the cause. I could do only a little, but I did it joyfully; I was happiest when attending an anti-slavery meeting. I seldom said much at the meetings because what I wanted to say was said better by others.

But at an anti-slavery convention in Nantucket on August 11, 1841, I felt strongly moved to speak. William C. Coffin, who had heard me speak at a black people's meeting in

New Bedford, encouraged me to do so. I was hesitant. I still thought of myself as a slave. The idea of speaking to whites intimidated me. But after I had spoken a few moments, I spoke freely and with ease.

From that time on, I have devoted myself to pleading the cause of my fellow slaves. I leave it to those acquainted with my efforts to decide my degree of success.

# APPENDIX

Having read over my story, I realize that some of what I have written might lead readers to mistake me for an enemy of all religion. What I have said against religion applies only to the religion of slaveholders and those in league with them, not to Christianity itself; I recognize the greatest possible difference between the two. Because I love the pure, peaceable Christianity of Christ, I hate the corrupt, cruel Christianity of those who support slavery. Indeed, I see no reason, except deception, to call such a religion Christianity.

I loathe the horrible hypocrisy of slaveholders' "Christianity." Slaveholding communities have cradle-robbers for church members, women-whippers for missionaries, and men-stealers for ministers. People who wield the blood-clotted whip during the week stand in the pulpit on Sunday, claiming to be ministers of meek, lowly Jesus. People who rob slaves of their earnings appear as teachers on Sunday morning, instructing slaves about the path to salvation. People who sell slave women for the purposes of prostitution call themselves pious advocates of purity. People who proclaim it a religious duty to read the Bible deny slaves the right to learn to read the word of God. Religious advocates of marriage rob millions of its sacred influence. Defenders of the sacredness of family, scatter families, tearing apart husbands and wives, parents and children, and sisters and brothers. Thieves preach against theft, and adulterers against adultery. Money used to build churches, support preaching, and purchase Bibles is acquired through the sale of women, men, and babies. Slaveholders insist on religion's outward forms while ignoring weighty matters of judgment, mercy, and faith.

I earnestly hope that this little book will throw light on the American slave system and hasten the glad day of deliverance of my millions of brothers and sisters who are in bonds. I rely on the power of truth, love, and justice and solemnly pledge myself anew to the sacred cause.

*Frederick Douglass*
*Lynn, Massachusetts, April 28, 1845*

# AFTERWORD

## About the Author

When Frederick Douglass ends his *Narrative*, he is a young married man of about 24, newly arrived in the free state of Massachusetts, and just beginning to be known as a public speaker. He closes his book by saying that he is "pleading the cause of my fellow slaves. I leave it to those acquainted with my efforts to decide my degree of success."

How successful was Douglass in "pleading the cause"? The fact is that the publication of the *Narrative of the Life of Frederick Douglass* made its author a famous and influential man. It put him in the spotlight, and that, at first, was not a comfortable position for him. But let's back up a little and fill in some important gaps in Douglass' story.

First of all, how did he escape from slavery? As Douglass explained in his *Narrative*, he could not provide details without getting other people in trouble. But years later, after slavery was abolished in the United States, he did publish the story of his escape.

In Baltimore, he had become friends with a free black man, a sailor named Benny. Benny offered to lend his own identity papers to Douglass for his journey North. Now, using the papers was very dangerous for both Douglass and Benny. Benny could be arrested for helping Douglass, and Douglass, of course, would be returned to slavery if he were caught. To make matters worse, Benny and Douglass looked nothing alike, and Benny's papers included a description of their owner.

Taking Benny's papers, Douglass dressed as a sailor and boarded a train headed north. Thanks to his work in the shipyards, Douglass could "talk the talk" of a sailor, and he managed to escape suspicion. His papers were checked several times, but not carefully. He even met several white people who knew him as a slave in Baltimore, but dressed in his sailor's clothing, they didn't give him a second glance. Still feeling miserably anxious, he rode the train from Baltimore into Delaware, also a slave state. There he boarded a boat to Philadelphia, and from there took another train to New York, where he picks up his story again in the *Narrative*.

It was in 1841 that Douglass spoke at a meeting of the Massachusetts Antislavery Society, describing what freedom meant to him. The society was so impressed that it immediately hired him to lecture about his experience as a slave. Audiences were spellbound by Douglass, who was by all accounts a powerful public speaker. Some pro-slavery writers, worried about the publicity Douglass was receiving, accused him of being a fraud. They said he was "too literate" and "too articulate" to have ever really been a slave. To prove them wrong, Douglass wrote his *Narrative*, in which he provided names, dates, and places related to his days spent in slavery.

The book was an instant sensation, eventually selling over 30,000 copies in the United States and Britain. It was translated into French, German, and Dutch. While Douglass was happy that the book raised people's awareness of the horrors of slavery, its publication also put him in a frightening position. Now everyone knew that he was an escaped slave and that under Maryland law, he was the property of his old master. Any slavehunter could have captured him, forced him to return to Maryland, and collected a reward. To avoid capture, Douglass fled to Europe in August 1845. He spent the next 20 months on a lecture tour of England, Scotland, and Ireland. During that time, anti-slavery groups in England raised enough money to purchase his freedom.

When Douglass could safely return to the U.S., he moved to Rochester, New York. There he founded the *North Star*, an anti-slavery newspaper. His reputation as a spokesman for African Americans kept him in the public eye for the rest of his life. He organized a protest against segregated schools in Rochester. His home was a stop on the "underground railroad," the network that helped runaway slaves reach safety in the North. When the Civil War began in 1861, President Abraham Lincoln met Douglass twice to discuss the role of black soldiers in the Union Army. In 1877, President Rutherford Hayes appointed Douglass U.S. Marshal for the District of Columbia. He later served as U.S. minister to Haiti.

Throughout his long life, Douglass remained a fiery spokesman for racial equality. He also became involved in the fight for women's rights, becoming friends with many of the leading feminists of his day. On

February 20, 1895, he attended a meeting of the National Council of Women in Washington, D.C. , where the audience gave him a standing ovation. Shortly after returning home that day, he had a heart attack and died.

After his death, a eulogy for Frederick Douglass was presented by the Rev. Alexander Crummell, a well-known black activist of the time. Rev. Crummell's words are a fitting close to a discussion of Douglass' life. He wrote: "What use are we to make of such a character as Frederick Douglass? Let his life be a lesson to all our children. Let his virtues be rehearsed to future generations. Let not one of us forget to hold him up as a pattern for young men in any station of life."

## About the Book

Today, very few people would defend the institution of slavery. We take for granted that owning people is an evil, immoral practice. Why, then, should anybody bother to read the *Narrative of the Life of Frederick Douglass*? Slavery was wrong; slavery was awful; most importantly, slavery was abolished in the United States in 1865. Can't we just forget about it?

Just forgetting about it sounds tempting. Slavery isn't a pleasant subject to think about. If you're African American yourself, it probably angers you to think that your ancestors may have been held in slavery. If you are white, you may resent feeling blamed for something that happened long before you were born. Whoever you are, you might tend to think, "Let's focus on the future, not the past. It's time to move on."

By re-issuing this *Narrative*, are we aiming to re-open the wounds of slavery, stirring up anger and bitterness among us? No. The problem is, people don't really "move on" from a situation until they've understood it. If you and a close friend have a serious disagreement, for instance, you might be reluctant to talk honestly about it. So instead, you might put on a smiling face and say, "Let's just forget about it." But do you really forget about it? Or do your feelings about what happened stay raw and painful, ready to flare up again when something else—even something unimportant—happens between you?

The same dynamic is at work when you consider events that have happened between groups of people. A famous philosopher once said, "Those who cannot remember the past are condemned to repeat it." In other words, history is full of stories of people—and nations—making terrible mistakes. We can learn valuable lessons from those mistakes, and live more wisely as a result. Or we can ignore the lessons of history, saying, "That has nothing to do with me," and run the risk of repeating those terrible errors.

What sort of lessons does the *Narrative of the Life of Frederick Douglass* offer? First and most obviously, it helps correct misconceptions we might have about slavery. Most people don't really know much about the day-to-day life of American slaves. We may have read stories or watched movies in which slaves appear, but such characters are not usually the focus of the story—they're just in the background, going about their work. They may even appear to be happy and content. By contrast, Frederick Douglass gives us a very realistic description of slave life. He tells us about the atmosphere of violence: the beatings, whippings, rapes, and even murders that were ever-present threats. He describes the hunger, lack of adequate clothing and shelter, and inhumane working conditions that slaves endured. He tells us of the anguish slaves felt when they were ripped away from their families and friends. Perhaps most powerfully, he makes us feel the hopelessness and humiliation of a slave's daily life. Douglass makes us realize that even if a slave's master was relatively kind, like Mr. Freeland, he was still owned like a stick of furniture. Instead of being able to make his own decisions and plans, like a responsible adult, he was forced to live like a dependent child forever. Faced with the prospect of such a life, a slave had few options. He could sink into passive acceptance, sleepwalking his way through life. Or he, like Douglass, could be driven nearly mad with despair, tortured with thoughts of a freedom that would never be his—unless he were willing to risk his life for it.

More unexpectedly, Douglass's *Narrative* teaches us about the effect slavery had upon the people who benefited from it. It's easy for a reader today, when thinking about slaveholders, to say, "I could never be like that. If I had been born a slave owner, I would have been kind and humane. I would have freed my slaves. I would have seen how unjust slavery was, and I would have worked to change the system." After reading Douglass, that same modern person might question whether that is true. After all, slave owners were not a special breed of cruel, hateful people. They were ordinary men and women who grew up in a society that taught them that slavery was necessary and useful—even that they had a duty to uphold the traditions of slavery. And as Douglass illustrates, that teaching was seductive. It could change even someone like Mrs. Auld, "a woman of the kindest heart and feelings," into "a demon." She was changed, Douglass explains, by "[t]he fatal poison of irresponsible power." In other words, Mrs. Auld was destroyed, in a moral sense, when she was given unearned, God-like power over another human being. Douglass shows us that such power inevitably has evil consequences.

So what do these lessons matter in the 21st century? Slavery has been abolished in the United States (although it still exists in some parts of the world); it's hardly imaginable that it would ever be made legal again. What, then, does the story of Frederick Douglass have to teach us?

It's just this: While slavery is an ugly thing of the past, it existed as long as it did because people could find ways to dehumanize other fellow human beings; to see them as somehow less deserving, less worthwhile, less valuable than themselves. Today when we read Douglass's *Narrative*, it is clear that we are reading the words of an intelligent, sensitive person of great insight and compassion. It horrifies us to think that this man was treated for many years as a stupid beast of burden, valued only for his ability to do manual labor. But are we so different from Douglass's "masters"? A look at any day's headlines will show us that while the laws may have changed, human nature has not. We are still filled with the desire to dehumanize people who are somehow different from ourselves, in order to excuse ourselves for treating them badly.

Instead of seeing our common humanity, we focus on our different skin colors, different religions, different levels of education, different dates of arrival in this country, different sexual orientations, or different languages. We reserve our concern and humane treatment for people who are "like us."

We need the *Narrative of the Life of Frederick Douglass,* as much today as when it was published in 1845, to remind us of the infinite worth of every human being.